D1500420

All inquiries should be addressed to:

info@effortlessMath.com

www.EffortlessMath.com

**ISBN–13:** 978-1-970036-76-3

**ISBN–10:** 1-970036-76-1

**Published by: Effortless Math Education**

www.EffortlessMath.com

# Welcome to

# TASC Math Prep

## 2021

Thank you for choosing Effortless Math for your TASC Math test preparation and congratulations on making the decision to take the TASC test! It's a remarkable move you are taking, one that shouldn't be diminished in any capacity. That's why you need to use every tool possible to ensure you succeed on the test with the highest possible score, and this extensive study guide is one such tool.

If math has never been a strong subject for you, **don't worry**! This book will help you prepare for (and even ACE) the TASC test's math section. As test day draws nearer, effective preparation becomes increasingly more important. Thankfully, you have this comprehensive study guide to help you get ready for the test. With this guide, you can feel confident that you will be more than ready for the TASC Math test when the time comes.

First and foremost, it is important to note that this book is a study guide and not a textbook. It is best read from cover to cover. Every lesson of this "self-guided math book" was carefully developed to ensure that you are making the most effective use of your time while preparing for the test. This up-to-date guide reflects the 2021 test guidelines and will put you on the right track to hone your math skills, overcome exam anxiety, and boost your confidence, so that you can have your best to succeed on the TASC Math test.

# www.EffortlessMath.com

... So Much More Online!

✓ FREE Math lessons

✓ More Math learning books!

✓ Mathematics Worksheets

✓ Online Math Tutors

**Need a PDF version of this book?**

Send email to: Info@EffortlessMath.com

# Ace the TASC Math in 30 Days

## The Ultimate Crash Course to Beat the TASC Math Test

By

Reza Nazari

& Ava Ross

**This study guide will**:

☑ Explain the format of the TASC Math test.

☑ Describe specific test-taking strategies that you can use on the test.

☑ Provide TASC Math test-taking tips.

☑ Review all TASC Math concepts and topics you will be tested on.

☑ Help you identify the areas in which you need to concentrate your study time.

☑ Offer exercises that help you develop the basic math skills you will learn in each section.

☑ Give **2 realistic and full-length practice tests** (featuring new question types) with detailed answers to help you measure your exam readiness and build confidence.

This resource contains everything you will ever need to succeed on the TASC Math test. You'll get in-depth instructions on every math topic as well as tips and techniques on how to answer each question type. You'll also get plenty of practice questions to boost your test-taking confidence.

In addition, in the following pages you'll find:

➢ **How to Use This Book Effectively** – This section provides you with step-by-step instructions on how to get the most out of this comprehensive study guide.

➢ **How to study for the TASC Math Test** – A six-step study program has been developed to help you make the best use of this book and prepare for your TASC Math test. Here you'll find tips and strategies to guide your study program and help you understand TASC Math and how to ace the test.

➢ **TASC Math Review** – Learn everything you need to know about the TASC Math test.

➢ **TASC Math Test-Taking Strategies** – Learn how to effectively put these recommended test-taking techniques into use for improving your TASC Math score.

➢ **Test Day Tips** – Review these tips to make sure you will do your best when the big day comes.

## Effortless Math's TASC Online Center

Effortless Math Online TASC Center offers a complete study program, including the following:

✓ Step-by-step instructions on how to prepare for the TASC Math test

✓ Numerous TASC Math worksheets to help you measure your math skills

✓ Complete list of TASC Math formulas

✓ Video lessons for all TASC Math topics

✓ Full-length TASC Math practice tests

✓ And much more...

**No Registration Required.**

Visit **effortlessmath.com/TASC** to find your online TASC Math resources.

# How to Use This Book Effectively

Look no further when you need a study guide to improve your math skills to succeed on the math portion of the TASC test. Each chapter of this comprehensive guide to the TASC Math will provide you with the knowledge, tools, and understanding needed for every topic covered on the test.

It's imperative that you understand each topic before moving onto another one, as that's the way to guarantee your success. Each chapter provides you with examples and a step-by-step guide of every concept to better understand the content that will be on the test. To get the best possible results from this book:

➤ **Begin studying long before your test date**. This provides you ample time to learn the different math concepts. The earlier you begin studying for the test, the sharper your skills will be. Do not procrastinate! Provide yourself with plenty of time (at least 30 days) to learn the concepts and feel comfortable that you understand them when your test date arrives.

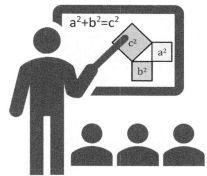

➤ **Practice consistently**. Study TASC Math concepts at least 20 to 30 minutes a day. Remember, slow and steady wins the race, which can be applied to preparing for the TASC Math test. Instead of cramming to tackle everything at once, be patient and learn the math topics in short bursts.

➤ Whenever you get a math problem wrong, **mark it off, and review it later** to make sure you understand the concept.

➤ Start each session by **looking over the previous material.**

➤ Once you've reviewed the book's lessons, **take a practice test on Day 29** to gauge your level of readiness. Then, review your results. Read detailed answers and solutions for each question you missed.

➤ **Take another practice test** (on Day 30) to get an idea of how ready you are to take the actual exam. Taking the practice tests will give you the confidence you need on test day. Simulate the TASC testing environment by sitting in a quiet room free from distraction. Make sure to clock yourself with a timer.

# How to Study for the TASC Math Test

Studying for the TASC Math test can be a really daunting and boring task. What's the best way to go about it? Is there a certain study method that works better than others? Well, studying for the TASC Math can be done effectively. The following six-step program has been designed to make preparing for the TASC Math test more efficient and less overwhelming.

Step **1** - Create a study plan
Step **2** - Choose your study resources
Step **3** - Review, Learn, Practice
Step **4** - Learn and practice test-taking strategies
Step **5** - Learn the TASC Test format and take practice tests
Step **6** - Analyze your performance

## STEP 1: Create a Study Plan

It's always easier to get things done when you have a plan. Creating a study plan for the TASC Math test can help you to stay on track with your studies. It's important to sit down and prepare a study plan with what works with your life, work, and any other obligations you may have. Devote enough time each day to studying. It's also a great

idea to break down each section of the exam into blocks and study one concept at a time.

It's important to understand that there is no "right" way to create a study plan. Your study plan will be personalized based on your specific needs and learning style.

Follow these guidelines to create an effective study plan for your TASC Math test:

★ **Analyze your learning style and study habits** – Everyone has a different learning style. It is essential to embrace your individuality and the unique way you learn. Think about what works and what doesn't work for you. Do you prefer TASC Math prep books or a combination of textbooks and video lessons? Does it work better for you if you study every night for thirty minutes or is it more effective to study in the morning before going to work?

★ **Evaluate your schedule** – Review your current schedule and find out how much time you can consistently devote to TASC Math study.

★ **Develop a schedule** – Now it's time to add your study schedule to your calendar like any other obligation. Schedule time for study, practice, and review. Plan out which topic you will study on which day to ensure that you're devoting enough time to each concept. Develop a study plan that is mindful, realistic, and flexible.

★ **Stick to your schedule** – A study plan is only effective when it is followed consistently. You should try to develop a study plan that you can follow for the length of your study program.

★ **Evaluate your study plan and adjust as needed** – Sometimes you need to adjust your plan when you have new commitments. Check in with yourself regularly to make sure that you're not falling behind in your study plan. Remember, the most important thing is sticking to your plan. Your study plan is all about helping you be more productive. If you find that your study plan is not as effective as you want, don't get discouraged. It's okay to make changes as you figure out what works best for you.

## STEP 2: Choose Your Study Resources

There are numerous textbooks and online resources available for the TASC Math test, and it may not be clear where to begin. Don't worry! This study guide provides everything you need to fully prepare for your TASC Math test. In addition to the book content, you can also use

Effortless Math's online resources. (video lessons, worksheets, formulas, etc.)

Simply visit effortlessmath.com/TASC to find your online TASC Math resources.

## STEP 3: Review, Learn, Practice

This TASC Math study guide breaks down each subject into specific skills or content areas. For instance, the percent concept is separated into different topics–percent calculation, percent increase and decrease, percent problems, etc. Use this book to help you go over all key math concepts and topics on the TASC Math test.

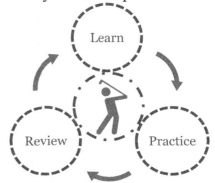

As you read each chapter, take notes or highlight the concepts you would like to go over again in the future. If you're unfamiliar with a topic or something is difficult for you, do additional research on it. For each math topic, plenty of instructions, step-by-step guides, and examples are provided to ensure you get a good grasp of the material. You can also find video lessons on the Effortless Math website for each TASC Math concept.

Quickly review the topics you do understand to get a brush-up of the material. Be sure to do the practice questions provided at the end of every chapter to measure your understanding of the concepts.

## STEP 4: Learn and Practice Test-taking Strategies

In the following sections, you will find important test-taking strategies and tips that can help you earn extra points. You'll learn how to think strategically and when to guess if you don't know the answer to a question. Using TASC Math test-taking strategies and tips can help you raise your score and do well on the test. Apply test taking strategies on the practice tests to help you boost your confidence.

## STEP 5: Learn the TASC Test Format and Take Practice Tests

The TASC *Test Review* section provides information about the structure of the TASC test. Read this section to learn more about the TASC test structure, different test sections, the number of questions in each section, and the section time limits. When you have a prior understanding of the test format and different types of TASC Math questions, you'll feel more confident when you take the actual exam.

Once you have read through the instructions and lessons and feel like you are ready to go – take advantage of both of the full-length TASC Math practice tests available in this study guide on Days 29 and 30. Use the practice tests to sharpen your skills and build confidence.

The TASC Math practice tests offered at the end of the book are formatted similarly to the actual TASC Math test. When you take each practice test, try to simulate actual testing conditions. To take the practice tests, sit in a quiet space, time yourself, and work through as many of the questions as time allows. The practice tests are followed by detailed answer explanations to help you find your weak areas, learn from your mistakes, and raise your TASC Math score.

## STEP 6: Analyze Your Performance

After taking the practice tests, look over the answer keys and explanations to learn which questions you answered correctly and which you did not. Never be discouraged if you make a few mistakes. See them as a learning opportunity. This will highlight your strengths and weaknesses.

You can use the results to determine if you need additional practice or if you are ready to take the actual TASC Math test.

# Looking for more?

Visit effortlessmath.com/TASC to find hundreds of TASC Math worksheets, video tutorials, practice tests, TASC Math formulas, and much more.

Or scan this QR code.

**No Registration Required.**

# TASC Test Review

The Test Assessing Secondary Completion, commonly known as the TASC or high school equivalency degree, is a standardized test. The TASC is a standardized test to verify that examinees have knowledge in core content areas equivalent to that of graduating high school seniors.

There are five subject area tests on TASC:

- Reading;
- Writing;
- Social Studies;
- Science;
- Mathematics.

The TASC Mathematics test is a 105-minute test that covers basic mathematics topics, quantitative problem-solving and algebraic questions. There are two Mathematics sections on the TASC. The first section contains 40 multiple choice questions where calculators are permitted. You have 55 minutes to complete this section. The second section contains 12 Gridded-Response questions. Calculator is NOT allowed in the second part. Test takers have 50 minutes to answer all questions in this section. Examinees will also be given a page of mathematic formulas to use during the test.

# TASC Math Test-Taking Strategies

Here are some test-taking strategies that you can use to maximize your performance and results on the TASC Math test.

## #1 : USE THIS APPROACH TO ANSWER EVERY TASC MATH QUESTION

- Review the question to identify keywords and important information.
- Translate the keywords into math operations so you can solve the problem.
- Review the answer choices. What are the differences between answer choices?
- Draw or label a diagram if needed.
- Try to find patterns.
- Find the right method to answer the question. Use straightforward math, plug in numbers, or test the answer choices (backsolving).
- Double-check your work.

## #2 : USE EDUCATED GUESSING

This approach is applicable to the problems you understand to some degree but cannot solve using straightforward math. In such cases, try to filter out as many answer choices as possible before picking an answer. In cases where you don't have a clue about what a certain problem entails, don't waste any time trying to eliminate answer choices. Just choose one randomly before moving onto the next question.

As you can ascertain, direct solutions are the most optimal approach. Carefully read through the question, determine what the solution is using the math you have learned before, then coordinate the answer with one of the choices available to you. Are you stumped? Make your best guess, then move on.

Don't leave any fields empty! Even if you're unable to work out a problem, strive to answer it. Take a guess if you have to. You will not lose points by getting an answer wrong, though you may gain a point by getting it correct!

# #3 : BALLPARK

A ballpark answer is a rough approximation. When we become overwhelmed by calculations and figures, we end up making silly mistakes. A decimal that is moved by one unit can change an answer from right to wrong, regardless of the number of steps that you went through to get it. That's where ballparking can play a big part.

If you think you know what the correct answer may be (even if it's just a ballpark answer), you'll usually have the ability to eliminate a couple of choices. While answer choices are usually based on the average student error and/or values that are closely tied, you will still be able to weed out choices that are way far afield. Try to find answers that aren't in the proverbial ballpark when you're looking for a wrong answer on a multiple-choice question. This is an optimal approach to eliminating answers to a problem.

# #4 : BACKSOLVING

A majority of questions on the TASC Math test will be in multiple-choice format. Many test-takers prefer multiple-choice questions, as at least the answer is right there. You'll typically have four answers to pick from. You simply need to figure out which one is correct. Usually, the best way to go about doing so is "backsolving."

As mentioned earlier, direct solutions are the most optimal approach to answering a question. Carefully read through a problem, calculate a solution, then correspond the answer with one of the choices displayed in front of you. If you can't calculate a solution, your next best approach involves "backsolving."

When backsolving a problem, contrast one of your answer options against the problem you are asked, then see which of them is most relevant. More often than not, answer choices are listed in ascending or descending order. In such cases, try out the choices B or C. If it's not correct, you can go either down or up from there.

# #5 : PLUGGING IN NUMBERS

"Plugging in numbers" is a strategy that can be applied to a wide range of different math problems on the TASC Math test. This approach is typically used to simplify a challenging question so that it is more understandable. By using the strategy carefully, you can find the answer without too much trouble.

The concept is fairly straightforward—replace unknown variables in a problem with certain values. When selecting a number, consider the following:

- Choose a number that's basic (just not too basic). Generally, you should avoid choosing 1 (or even 0). A decent choice is 2.

- Try not to choose a number that is displayed in the problem.

- Make sure you keep your numbers different if you need to choose at least two of them.

- More often than not, choosing numbers merely lets you filter out some of your answer choices. As such, don't just go with the first choice that gives you the right answer.

- If several answers seem correct, then you'll need to choose another value and try again. This time, though, you'll just need to check choices that haven't been eliminated yet.

- If your question contains fractions, then a potential right answer may involve either an LCD (least common denominator) or an LCD multiple.

- 100 is the number you should choose when you are dealing with problems involving percentages.

# TASC Mathematics Test – Daytime Tips

After practicing and reviewing all the math concepts you've been taught, and taking some TASC mathematics practice tests, you'll be prepared for test day. Consider the following tips to be extra-ready come test time.

**Before Your Test** ........................................................................................................

What to do the night before:

- **Relax!** One day before your test, study lightly or skip studying altogether. You shouldn't attempt to learn something new, either. There are plenty of reasons why studying the evening before a big test can work against you. Put it this way–a marathoner wouldn't go out for a sprint before the day of a big race. Mental marathoners–such as yourself–should not study for any more than one hour 24 hours before a TASC test. That's because your brain requires some rest to be at its best. The night before your exam, spend some time with family or friends, or read a book.

- **Avoid bright screens** - You'll have to get some good shuteye the night before your test. Bright screens (such as the ones coming from your laptop, TV, or mobile device) should be avoided altogether. Staring at such a screen will keep your brain up, making it hard to drift asleep at a reasonable hour.

- **Make sure your dinner is healthy** - The meal that you have for dinner should be nutritious. Be sure to drink plenty of water as well. Load up on your complex carbohydrates, much like a marathon runner would do. Pasta, rice, and potatoes are ideal options here, as are vegetables and protein sources.

- **Get your bag ready for test day** - The night prior to your test, pack your bag with your stationery, admissions pass, ID, and any other gear that you need. Keep the bag right by your front door.

- **Make plans to reach the testing site** - Before going to sleep, ensure that you understand precisely how you will arrive at the site of the test. If parking is something you'll have to find first, plan for it. If you're dependent on public transit, then review the schedule. You should also make sure that the train/bus/subway/streetcar you use will be running. Find out about road closures as well. If a parent or friend is accompanying you, ensure that they understand what steps they have to take as well.

## The Day of the Test

- **Get up reasonably early, but not too early.**

- **Have breakfast** - Breakfast improves your concentration, memory, and mood. As such, make sure the breakfast that you eat in the morning is healthy. The last thing you want to be is distracted by a grumbling tummy. If it's not your own stomach making those noises, another test taker close to you might be instead. Prevent discomfort or embarrassment by consuming a healthy breakfast. Bring a snack with you if you think you'll need it.

- **Follow your daily routine** - Do you watch Good Morning America each morning while getting ready for the day? Don't break your usual habits on the day of the test. Likewise, if coffee isn't something you drink in the morning, then don't take up the habit hours before your test. Routine consistency lets you concentrate on the main objective–doing the best you can on your test.

- **Wear layers** - Dress yourself up in comfortable layers. You should be ready for any kind of internal temperature. If it gets too warm during the test, take a layer off.

- **Get there on time** - The last thing you want to do is get to the test site late. Rather, you should be there 45 minutes prior to the start of the test. Upon your arrival, try not to hang out with anybody who is nervous. Any anxious energy they exhibit shouldn't influence you.

- **Leave the books at home** - No books should be brought to the test site. If you start developing anxiety before the test, books could encourage you to do some last-minute studying, which will only hinder you. Keep the books far away–better yet, leave them at home.

- **Make your voice heard** - If something is off, speak to a proctor. If medical attention is needed or if you'll require anything, consult the proctor prior to the start of the test. Any doubts you have should be clarified. You should be entering the test site with a state of mind that is completely clear.

■ **Have faith in yourself** - When you feel confident, you will be able to perform at your best. When you are waiting for the test to begin, envision yourself receiving an outstanding result. Try to see yourself as someone who knows all the answers, no matter what the questions are. A lot of athletes tend to use this technique—particularly before a big competition. Your expectations will be reflected by your performance.

## During your test

■ **Be calm and breathe deeply** - You need to relax before the test, and some deep breathing will go a long way to help you do that. Be confident and calm. You got this. Everybody feels a little stressed out just before an evaluation of any kind is set to begin. Learn some effective breathing exercises. Spend a minute meditating before the test starts. Filter out any negative thoughts you have. Exhibit confidence when having such thoughts.

■ **Concentrate on the test** - Refrain from comparing yourself to anyone else. You shouldn't be distracted by the people near you or random noise. Concentrate exclusively on the test. If you find yourself irritated by surrounding noises, earplugs can be used to block sounds off close to you. Don't forget—the test is going to last several hours if you're taking more than one subject of the test. Some of that time will be dedicated to brief sections. Concentrate on the specific section you are working on during a particular moment. Do not let your mind wander off to upcoming or previous sections.

■ **Skip challenging questions** - Optimize your time when taking the test. Lingering on a single question for too long will work against you. If you don't know what the answer is to a certain question, use your best guess, and mark the question so you can review it later on. There is no need to spend time attempting to solve something you aren't sure about. That time would be better served handling the questions you can actually answer well. You will not be penalized for getting the wrong answer on a test like this.

■ **Try to answer each question individually** - Focus only on the question you are working on. Use one of the test-taking strategies to solve the problem. If you aren't able to come up with an answer, don't get frustrated. Simply skip that question, then move onto the next one.

■ **Don't forget to breathe!** Whenever you notice your mind wandering, your stress levels boosting, or frustration brewing, take a thirty-second break. Shut your eyes, drop your pencil, breathe deeply, and let your shoulders relax. You will end up being more productive when you allow yourself to relax for a moment.

■ **Review your answer.** If you still have time at the end of the test, don't waste it. Go back and check over your answers. It is worth going through the test from start to finish to ensure that you didn't make a sloppy mistake somewhere.

■ **Optimize your breaks** - When break time comes, use the restroom, have a snack, and reactivate your energy for the subsequent section. Doing some stretches can help stimulate your blood flow.

## After your test

■ **Take it easy** - You will need to set some time aside to relax and decompress once the test has concluded. There is no need to stress yourself out about what you could've said, or what you may have done wrong. At this point, there's nothing you can do about it. Your energy and time would be better spent on something that will bring you happiness for the remainder of your day.

■ **Redoing the test** - Did you pass the test? Congratulations! Your hard work paid off! Passing this test means that you are now as knowledgeable as somebody who has graduated high school.

If you have failed your test, though, don't worry! The test can be retaken. In such cases, you will need to follow the retake policy established by your state. You also need to re-register to take the exam again.

# contents

# Day 1: Whole Numbers

**Math Topics that you'll learn today:**

- ✓ Rounding
- ✓ Whole Number Addition and Subtraction
- ✓ Whole Number Multiplication and Division
- ✓ Rounding and Estimates

*"If people do not believe that mathematics is simple, it is only because they do not realize how complicated life is."*
*— John von Neumann*

# Rounding

**Step-by-step guide:**

Rounding is putting a number up or down to the nearest whole number or the nearest hundred, etc.

✓ First, find the place value you'll round to.
✓ Find the digit to the right of the place value you're rounding to. If it is 5 or

bigger, add 1 to the place value you're rounding to and put zero for all digits

on its right side. If the digit to the right of the place value is less than 5,

keep the place value and put zero for all digits to the right.

**Examples:**

1) Round **64** to the nearest ten.

The place value of ten is 6. The digit on the right side is 4 (which is less than 5). Keep 6 and put zero for the digit on the right side. The answer is 60. 64 rounded to the nearest ten is 60, because 64 is closer to 60 than to 70.

2) Round **694** to the nearest hundred.

694 rounded to the nearest hundred is 700, because the digit on the right side of hundred place is 9. Add 1 to 6 and put zeros for other digits. The answer is 700.

✎ *Round each number to the nearest ten.*

1) 84 = ____          4) 63 = ____
2) 70 = ____          5) 79 = ____
3) 47 = ____          6) 55 = ____

✎ *Round each number to the nearest hundred.*

7)  185 = ____        10)  109 = ____
8)  254 = ____        11)  222 = ____
9)  729 = ____        12)  311 = ____

# Whole Number Addition and Subtraction

**Step-by-step guide:**

- ✓ Line up the numbers.
- ✓ Start with the unit place. (ones place)
- ✓ Regroup if necessary.
- ✓ Add or subtract the tens place.
- ✓ Continue with other digits.

**Examples:**

1) Find the sum. $285 + 145 = ?$

First line up the numbers: $\begin{array}{r} 285 \\ + 145 \\ \hline \end{array}$ → Start with the unit place. (ones place) $5 + 5 = 10$,

Write 0 for ones place and keep 1, $\begin{array}{r} \scriptstyle 1 \\ 285 \\ + 145 \\ \hline 0 \end{array}$ , Add the tens place and the digit 1 we kept:

$1 + 8 + 4 = 13$, Write 3 and keep 1, $\begin{array}{r} \scriptstyle 1\ 1 \\ 285 \\ + 145 \\ \hline 30 \end{array}$

Continue with other digits → $1 + 2 + 1 = 4$ → $\begin{array}{r} \scriptstyle 1\ 1 \\ 285 \\ + 145 \\ \hline 430 \end{array}$

2) Find the difference. $976 - 453 = ?$

First line up the numbers: $\begin{array}{r} 976 \\ - 453 \\ \hline \end{array}$ , → Start with the unit place. $6 - 3 = 3$, $\begin{array}{r} 976 \\ - 453 \\ \hline 3 \end{array}$,

Subtract the tens place. $7 - 5 = 2$, $\begin{array}{r} 976 \\ - 453 \\ \hline 23 \end{array}$ , Continue with other digits → $9 - 4 = 5$, $\begin{array}{r} 976 \\ - 453 \\ \hline 523 \end{array}$

✎ *Find the sum or difference.*

1) $1,264 + 856 =$

2) $2,689 - 456 =$

3) $1,432 - 556 =$

4) $2,820 + 464 =$

5) $2,170 + 245 =$

6) $3,221 + 2,560 =$

7) $3,788 + 1,892 =$

8) $4,238 + 2,576 =$

# Whole Number Multiplication

**Step-by-step guide:**

- ✓ Learn the times tables first! To solve multiplication problems fast, you need to memorize the times table. For example, 3 times 8 is 24 or 8 times 7 is 56.
- ✓ For multiplication, line up the numbers you are multiplying.
- ✓ Start with the ones place and regroup if necessary.
- ✓ Continue with other digits.

**Examples:**

**1)** Solve. $500 \times 30 = ?$

Line up the numbers: $\begin{array}{r} 500 \\ \times\,30 \\ \hline \end{array}$ , start with the ones place → $0 \times 500 = 0$, $\begin{array}{r} 500 \\ \times\,30 \\ \hline 0 \end{array}$ , Continue

with other digit which is 3. → $500 \times 3 = 1,500$, $\begin{array}{r} 500 \\ \times\,30 \\ \hline 1,5000 \end{array}$

**2)** Solve. $820 \times 25 = ?$

Line up the numbers: $\begin{array}{r} 820 \\ \times\,25 \\ \hline \end{array}$ , start with the ones place → $5 \times 0 = 0$, $\begin{array}{r} 820 \\ \times\,25 \\ \hline 0 \end{array}$, $5 \times 2 = 10$,

write 0 and keep 1. $\begin{array}{r} 820 \\ \times\,25 \\ \hline 00 \end{array}$, → $5 \times 8 = 40$, add 1 to 40, the answer is 41. $\begin{array}{r} 820 \\ \times\,25 \\ \hline 4,100 \end{array}$

Now, write 0 in the next line and multiply 820 by 2, using the same process. (Since 2 is in the tens place, we need to write 0 before doing the operation). The answer is 16,400. Add 4,100 and 16,400. The answer is: $4,100 + 16,400 = 20,500$

## ✎ Find the missing number.

1) $24 \times 5 = $ _____
2) $28 \times 8 = $ _____
3) $360 \times 6 = $ _____
4) $500 \times 12 = $ _____

5) $144 \times 51 = $ _____
6) $238 \times 18 = $ _____
7) $362 \times 14 = $ _____
8) $238 \times 28 = $ _____

# Whole Number Division

## Step-by-step guide:

Division: A typical division problem: Dividend ÷ Divisor = Quotient

- In division, we want to find how many times a number (divisor) is contained in another number (dividend). The result in a division problem is the quotient.
- ✓ First, write the problem in division format. (dividend is inside; divisor is outside)

$$\overset{\text{Quotient}}{\text{Divisor} \overline{)\text{Dividend}}}$$

- ✓ Now, find how many times divisor goes into dividend. (if it is a big number, break the dividend into smaller numbers by choosing the appropriate number of digits from left. Start from the first digit on the left side of the divided and see if the divisor will go into it. If not, keep moving over one digit to the right in the dividend until you have a number the divisor will go into.
- ✓ Find number of times the divisor goes into the part of the dividend you chose.
- ✓ Write the answer above the digit in the dividend you are using and multiply it by the divisor and Write the product under the part of the dividend you are using, then subtract.
- ✓ Bring down the next digit in the dividend and repeat this process until you have nothing left to bring down.

## Example: Solve. 234 ÷ 4 = ?

$$4\overline{)234}$$

- ✓ First, write the problem in division format.
- ✓ Start from left digit of the dividend. 4 doesn't go into 2. So, choose another digit of the dividend. It is 3.
- ✓ Now, find how many times 4 goes into 23. The answer is 5.
- ✓ Write 5 above the dividend part. 4 times 5 is 20. Write 20 below 23 and subtract. The answer is 3.

$$\overset{5}{4\overline{)234}}$$

- ✓ Now bring down the next digit which is 4. How many times 4 goes into 34? The answer is 8. Write 8 above dividend. This is the final step since there is no other digit of the dividend to bring down. The final answer is 58 and the remainder is 2.

$$\begin{array}{r} 58 \\ 4\overline{)234} \\ -20 \phantom{0}\\ \hline 34 \\ -32 \\ \hline 2 \end{array}$$

## ✍ Solve.

1) $240 \div 5 =$ _____
2) $280 \div 4 =$ _____
3) $562 \div 8 =$ _____
4) $522 \div 9 =$ _____

5) $834 \div 8 =$ _____
6) $922 \div 12 =$ _____
7) $880 \div 15 =$ _____
8) $721 \div 22 =$ _____

# Rounding and Estimates

**Step-by-step guide:**

Rounding and estimating are math strategies used for approximating a number. To estimate means to make a rough guess or calculation. To round means to simplify a known number by scaling it slightly up or down.

✓ To estimate a math operation, round the numbers.
✓ For 2 −digit numbers, your usually can round to the nearest tens, for 3 −digit numbers, round to nearest hundreds, etc.
✓ Find the answer.

**Examples:**

1) Estimate the sum by rounding each number to the nearest hundred. $153 + 426 =?$
   153 rounded to the nearest hundred is 200. 426 rounded to the nearest hundred is 400.
   Then: $200 + 400 = 600$

2) Estimate the result by rounding each number to the nearest ten. $38 - 26 = ?$
   38 rounded to the nearest ten is 40. 25 rounded to the nearest ten is 30.
   Then: $40 - 30 = 10$

✍ *Estimate the sum by rounding each number to the nearest ten.*

1) $14 + 68 =$ _____

2) $82 + 12 =$ _____

3) $43 + 66 =$ _____

4) $47 + 69 =$ _____

5) $553 + 231 =$ _____

6) $418 + 849 =$ _____

✍ *Estimate the product by rounding each number to the nearest ten.*

7) $55 \times 62 =$ _____

8) $14 \times 27 =$ _____

9) $34 \times 66 =$ _____

10) $18 \times 12 =$ _____

11) $62 \times 53 =$ _____

12) $41 \times 26 =$ _____

# Answers – Day 1

### Rounding

| | | |
|---|---|---|
| 1) 80 | 5) 80 | 9) 700 |
| 2) 70 | 6) 60 | 10) 100 |
| 3) 50 | 7) 200 | 11) 200 |
| 4) 60 | 8) 300 | 12) 300 |

### Whole Number Addition and Subtraction

| | | |
|---|---|---|
| 1) 2,120 | 4) 3,284 | 7) 5,680 |
| 2) 2,233 | 5) 2,415 | 8) 6,814 |
| 3) 876 | 6) 5,781 | |

### Whole Number Multiplication

| | | |
|---|---|---|
| 1) 120 | 4) 6,000 | 7) 5,068 |
| 2) 224 | 5) 7,344 | 8) 6,664 |
| 3) 2,160 | 6) 4,284 | |

### Whole Number Division

| | | |
|---|---|---|
| 1) 48 | 4) 58 | 7) $58, r10$ |
| 2) 70 | 5) $104, 2$ | 8) $32, 17$ |
| 3) $70, r2$ | 6) $76, r10$ | |

### Rounding and Estimates

| | | |
|---|---|---|
| 1) 80 | 5) 780 | 9) 2,100 |
| 2) 90 | 6) 1,270 | 10) 200 |
| 3) 110 | 7) 3,600 | 11) 3,000 |
| 4) 120 | 8) 300 | 12) 1,200 |

# Day 2: Fractions

**Math Topics that you'll learn today:**

- ✓ Comparing Numbers

- ✓ Simplifying Fractions

- ✓ Adding and Subtracting Fractions

- ✓ Multiplying and Dividing Fractions

*"A Man is like a fraction whose numerator is what he is and whose denominator is what he thinks of himself. The larger the denominator, the smaller the fraction." ~Tolstoy*

# Simplifying Fractions

**Step-by-step guide:**

✓ Evenly divide both the top and bottom of the fraction by $2, 3, 5, 7, \ldots$ etc.

✓ Continue until you can't go any further.

**Examples:**

1) Simplify $\frac{12}{20}$.

To simplify $\frac{12}{20}$, find a number that both 12 and 20 are divisible by. Both are divisible by 4.
Then: $\frac{12}{20} = \frac{12 \div 4}{20 \div 4} = \frac{3}{5}$

2) Simplify $\frac{64}{80}$.

To simplify $\frac{64}{80}$, find a number that both 64 and 80 are divisible by. Both are divisible by 8 and 16. Then: $\frac{64}{80} = \frac{64 \div 8}{80 \div 8} = \frac{8}{10}$, 8 and 10 are divisible by 2, then: $\frac{8}{10} = \frac{4}{5}$

or $\frac{64}{80} = \frac{64 \div 16}{80 \div 16} = \frac{4}{5}$

✎ *Simplify each fraction.*

1) $\frac{9}{18} =$

2) $\frac{8}{10} =$

3) $\frac{6}{8} =$

4) $\frac{5}{20} =$

5) $\frac{18}{24} =$

6) $\frac{6}{9} =$

7) $\frac{12}{15} =$

8) $\frac{4}{16} =$

9) $\frac{18}{36} =$

10) $\frac{6}{42} =$

11) $\frac{13}{39} =$

12) $\frac{21}{28} =$

## Adding and Subtracting Fractions

**Step-by-step guide:**

- ✓ For "like" fractions (fractions with the same denominator), add or subtract the numerators and write the answer over the common denominator.
- ✓ Find equivalent fractions with the same denominator before you can add or subtract fractions with different denominators.
- ✓ Adding and Subtracting with the same denominator:

$$\frac{a}{b} + \frac{c}{b} = \frac{a+c}{b} \ , \ \frac{a}{b} - \frac{c}{b} = \frac{a-c}{b}$$

- ✓ Adding and Subtracting fractions with different denominators:

$$\frac{a}{b} + \frac{c}{d} = \frac{ad+c}{bd} \ , \ \frac{a}{b} - \frac{c}{d} = \frac{ad-cb}{bd}$$

**Examples:**

1) Subtract fractions. $\frac{4}{5} - \frac{3}{5} =$

For "like" fractions, subtract the numerators and write the answer over the common denominator. then: $\frac{4}{5} - \frac{3}{5} = \frac{1}{5}$

2) Subtract fractions. $\frac{2}{3} - \frac{1}{2} =$

For "unlike" fractions, find equivalent fractions with the same denominator before you can add or subtract fractions with different denominators. Use this formula: $\frac{a}{b} - \frac{c}{d} = \frac{ad-cb}{bd}$

$\frac{2}{3} - \frac{1}{2} = \frac{(2)(2) - (1)(3)}{3 \times 2} = \frac{4-3}{6} = \frac{1}{6}$

✍ *Find the sum or difference.*

1) $\frac{1}{3} + \frac{2}{3} =$      4) $\frac{3}{7} + \frac{2}{3} =$      7) $\frac{2}{3} - \frac{1}{6} =$

2) $\frac{1}{2} + \frac{1}{3} =$      5) $\frac{1}{2} - \frac{1}{3} =$      8) $\frac{3}{5} - \frac{1}{2} =$

3) $\frac{2}{5} + \frac{1}{2} =$      6) $\frac{4}{5} - \frac{2}{3} =$      9) $\frac{8}{9} - \frac{2}{5} =$

# Multiplying and Dividing Fractions

**Step-by-step guide:**

✓ Multiplying fractions: multiply the top numbers and multiply the bottom numbers.
✓ Dividing fractions: Keep, Change, Flip
✓ Keep first fraction, change division sign to multiplication, and flip the numerator and denominator of the second fraction. Then, solve!

**Examples:**

1) Multiplying fractions. $\frac{5}{6} \times \frac{3}{4} =$

Multiply the top numbers and multiply the bottom numbers.

$\frac{5}{6} \times \frac{3}{4} = \frac{5 \times 3}{6 \times 4} = \frac{15}{24}$, simplify: $\frac{15}{24} = \frac{15 \div 3}{24 \div 3} = \frac{5}{8}$

2) Dividing fractions. $\frac{1}{4} \div \frac{2}{3} =$

Keep first fraction, change division sign to multiplication, and flip the numerator and denominator of the second fraction. Then: $\frac{1}{4} \times \frac{3}{2} = \frac{1 \times 3}{4 \times 2} = \frac{3}{8}$

✍ *Find the answers.*

1) $\frac{1}{2} \times \frac{3}{4} =$

2) $\frac{3}{5} \times \frac{2}{3} =$

3) $\frac{1}{4} \times \frac{2}{5} =$

4) $\frac{1}{6} \times \frac{4}{5} =$

5) $\frac{1}{5} \times \frac{1}{4} =$

6) $\frac{2}{5} \times \frac{1}{2} =$

7) $\frac{1}{2} \div \frac{1}{4} =$

8) $\frac{1}{3} \div \frac{1}{2} =$

9) $\frac{2}{5} \div \frac{1}{3} =$

10) $\frac{1}{4} \div \frac{2}{3} =$

11) $\frac{1}{5} \div \frac{3}{10} =$

12) $\frac{2}{7} \div \frac{1}{3} =$

# Answers – Day 2

## Simplifying Fractions

1) $\frac{1}{2}$

2) $\frac{4}{5}$

3) $\frac{3}{4}$

4) $\frac{1}{4}$

5) $\frac{3}{4}$

6) $\frac{2}{3}$

7) $\frac{4}{5}$

8) $\frac{1}{4}$

9) $\frac{1}{2}$

10) $\frac{1}{7}$

11) $\frac{1}{3}$

12) $\frac{3}{4}$

## Adding and Subtracting Fractions

1) $\frac{3}{3} = 1$

2) $\frac{5}{6}$

3) $\frac{9}{10}$

4) $\frac{23}{21}$

5) $\frac{1}{6}$

6) $\frac{2}{15}$

7) $\frac{1}{2}$

8) $\frac{1}{10}$

9) $\frac{22}{45}$

## Multiplying and Dividing Fractions

1) $\frac{3}{8}$

2) $\frac{2}{5}$

3) $\frac{1}{10}$

4) $\frac{2}{15}$

5) $\frac{1}{20}$

6) $\frac{1}{5}$

7) $2$

8) $\frac{2}{3}$

9) $\frac{6}{5}$

10) $\frac{3}{8}$

11) $\frac{2}{3}$

12) $\frac{6}{7}$

# Day 3: Mixed Numbers

**Math Topics that you'll learn today:**

- ✓ Adding Mixed Numbers

- ✓ Subtracting Mixed Numbers

- ✓ Multiplying Mixed Numbers

- ✓ Dividing Mixed Numbers

*"Wherever there is number, there is beauty." – Proclus*

# Adding Mixed Numbers

**Step-by-step guide:**

Use the following steps for both adding and subtracting mixed numbers.

- ✓ Add whole numbers of the mixed numbers.
- ✓ Add the fractions of each mixed number.
- ✓ Find the Least Common Denominator (LCD) if necessary.
- ✓ Add whole numbers and fractions.
- ✓ Write your answer in lowest terms.

**Examples:**

1) Add mixed numbers. $1\frac{3}{4} + 2\frac{3}{8} =$

Rewriting our equation with parts separated, $1 + \frac{3}{4} + 2 + \frac{3}{8}$, Solving the whole number parts $1 + 2 = 3$, Solving the fraction parts $\frac{3}{4} + \frac{3}{8}$, and rewrite to solve with the equivalent fractions.

$\frac{6}{8} + \frac{3}{8} = \frac{9}{8} = 1\frac{1}{8}$, then Combining the whole and fraction parts $3 + 1 + \frac{1}{8} = 4\frac{1}{8}$

2) Add mixed numbers. $1\frac{2}{3} + 4\frac{1}{6} =$

Rewriting our equation with parts separated, $1 + \frac{2}{3} + 4 + \frac{1}{6}$, Solving the whole number parts $1 + 4 = 5$, Solving the fraction parts $\frac{2}{3} + \frac{1}{6}$, and rewrite to solve with the equivalent fractions.

$\frac{4}{6} + \frac{1}{6} = \frac{5}{6}$, then Combining the whole and fraction parts $5 + \frac{5}{6} = 5\frac{5}{6}$

✎ *Find the sum.*

1) $2\frac{1}{2} + 1\frac{1}{3} =$

2) $6\frac{1}{2} + 3\frac{1}{2} =$

3) $2\frac{3}{8} + 3\frac{1}{8} =$

4) $4\frac{1}{2} + 1\frac{1}{4} =$

5) $1\frac{3}{7} + 1\frac{5}{14} =$

6) $6\frac{5}{12} + 3\frac{3}{4} =$

7) $5\frac{1}{2} + 8\frac{3}{4} =$

8) $3\frac{7}{8} + 3\frac{1}{3} =$

9) $3\frac{3}{9} + 7\frac{6}{11} =$

## Subtract Mixed Numbers

**Step-by-step guide:**

Use the following steps for both adding and subtracting mixed numbers.

✓ Subtract the whole number of second mixed number from whole number of the first mixed number.
✓ Subtract the second fraction from the first one.
✓ Find the Least Common Denominator (LCD) if necessary.
✓ Add the result of whole numbers and fractions.
✓ Write your answer in lowest terms.

**Examples:**

1) Subtract. $5\frac{2}{3} - 2\frac{1}{4} =$

Rewriting our equation with parts separated, $5 + \frac{2}{3} - 2 - \frac{1}{4}$

Solving the whole number parts $5 - 2 = 3$, Solving the fraction parts, $\frac{2}{3} - \frac{1}{4} = \frac{8-3}{12} = \frac{5}{12}$

Combining the whole and fraction parts, $3 + \frac{5}{12} = 3\frac{5}{12}$

2) Subtract. $3\frac{4}{5} - 1\frac{1}{2} =$

Rewriting our equation with parts separated, $3 + \frac{4}{5} - 1 - \frac{1}{2}$

Solving the whole number parts $3 - 1 = 2$, Solving the fraction parts, $\frac{4}{5} - \frac{1}{2} = \frac{8-5}{10} = \frac{3}{10}$

Combining the whole and fraction parts, $2 + \frac{3}{10} = 2\frac{3}{10}$

✍ *Find the difference.*

1) $3\frac{1}{3} - 1\frac{1}{3} =$

2) $4\frac{1}{2} - 3\frac{1}{2} =$

3) $5\frac{1}{2} - 2\frac{1}{4} =$

4) $6\frac{1}{6} - 5\frac{1}{3} =$

5) $8\frac{1}{2} - 1\frac{1}{10} =$

6) $9\frac{1}{2} - 2\frac{1}{4} =$

7) $9\frac{1}{5} - 5\frac{1}{6} =$

8) $14\frac{3}{10} - 13\frac{1}{3} =$

9) $19\frac{2}{3} - 11\frac{5}{8} =$

# Multiplying Mixed Numbers

**Step-by-step guide:**

- ✓ Convert the mixed numbers to improper fractions. (improper fraction is a fraction in which the top number is bigger than bottom number)
- ✓ Multiply fractions and simplify if necessary.

$$a\frac{c}{b} = a + \frac{c}{b} = \frac{ab+c}{b}$$

**Examples:**

1) Multiply mixed numbers. $3\frac{2}{3} \times 2\frac{1}{2} =$

Converting mixed numbers to fractions, $3\frac{2}{3} = \frac{11}{3}$ and $2\frac{1}{2} = \frac{5}{2}$.

$\frac{11}{3} \times \frac{5}{2}$, Applying the fractions formula for multiplication, $\frac{11\times5}{3\times2} = \frac{55}{6} = 9\frac{1}{6}$

2) Multiply mixed numbers. $4\frac{3}{5} \times 2\frac{1}{3} =$

Converting mixed numbers to fractions, $\frac{23}{5} \times \frac{7}{3}$, Applying the fractions formula for multiplication, $\frac{23\times7}{5\times3} = \frac{161}{15} = 10\frac{11}{15}$

✍ *Find the product.*

1) $4\frac{1}{3} \times 2\frac{1}{5} =$

2) $3\frac{1}{2} \times 3\frac{1}{4} =$

3) $5\frac{2}{5} \times 2\frac{1}{3} =$

4) $2\frac{1}{2} \times 1\frac{2}{9} =$

5) $3\frac{4}{7} \times 2\frac{3}{5} =$

6) $7\frac{2}{3} \times 2\frac{2}{3} =$

7) $9\frac{8}{9} \times 8\frac{3}{4} =$

8) $2\frac{4}{7} \times 5\frac{2}{9} =$

9) $5\frac{2}{5} \times 2\frac{3}{5} =$

10) $3\frac{5}{7} \times 3\frac{5}{6} =$

# Dividing Mixed Numbers

**Step-by-step guide:**

✓ Convert the mixed numbers to improper fractions.

✓ Divide fractions and simplify if necessary.

$$a\frac{c}{b} = a + \frac{c}{b} = \frac{ab + c}{b}$$

**Examples:**

1) Find the quotient. $2\frac{1}{2} \div 1\frac{1}{5} =$

Converting mixed numbers to fractions, $\frac{5}{2} \div \frac{6}{5}$ , Applying the fractions formula for multiplication, $\frac{5 \times 5}{2 \times 6} = \frac{25}{12} = 2\frac{1}{12}$

2) Find the quotient. $4\frac{3}{4} \div 3\frac{4}{5} =$

Converting mixed numbers to fractions, $\frac{19}{4} \div \frac{19}{5}$ , Applying the fractions formula for multiplication, $\frac{19 \times 5}{4 \times 19} = \frac{95}{76} = 1\frac{1}{4}$

✎ *Find the quotient.*

1) $1\frac{2}{3} \div 3\frac{1}{3} =$

2) $2\frac{1}{4} \div 1\frac{1}{2} =$

3) $10\frac{1}{2} \div 1\frac{2}{3} =$

4) $3\frac{1}{6} \div 4\frac{2}{3} =$

5) $4\frac{1}{8} \div 2\frac{1}{2} =$

6) $2\frac{1}{10} \div 2\frac{3}{5} =$

7) $1\frac{4}{11} \div 1\frac{1}{4} =$

8) $9\frac{1}{2} \div 9\frac{2}{3} =$

9) $8\frac{3}{4} \div 2\frac{2}{5} =$

10) $12\frac{1}{2} \div 9\frac{1}{3} =$

# Answers – Day 3

## Adding Mixed Numbers

1) $3\frac{5}{6}$

2) $10$

3) $5\frac{1}{2}$

4) $5\frac{3}{4}$

5) $2\frac{11}{14}$

6) $10\frac{1}{6}$

7) $14\frac{1}{4}$

8) $7\frac{5}{24}$

9) $10\frac{29}{33}$

## Subtract Mixed Numbers

1) $2$

2) $1$

3) $3\frac{1}{4}$

4) $\frac{5}{6}$

5) $7\frac{2}{5}$

6) $7\frac{1}{4}$

7) $4\frac{1}{30}$

8) $\frac{29}{30}$

9) $8\frac{1}{24}$

## Multiplying Mixed Numbers

1) $9\frac{8}{15}$

2) $11\frac{3}{8}$

3) $12\frac{3}{5}$

4) $3\frac{1}{18}$

5) $9\frac{2}{7}$

6) $20\frac{4}{9}$

7) $86\frac{19}{36}$

8) $13\frac{3}{7}$

9) $14\frac{1}{25}$

10) $14\frac{5}{21}$

## Dividing Mixed Numbers

1) $\frac{1}{2}$

2) $1\frac{1}{2}$

3) $6\frac{3}{10}$

4) $\frac{19}{28}$

5) $1\frac{13}{20}$

6) $\frac{21}{26}$

7) $1\frac{1}{11}$

8) $\frac{57}{58}$

9) $3\frac{31}{48}$

10) $1\frac{19}{56}$

# Day 4: Decimals

**Math Topics that you'll learn today:**

- ✓ Comparing Decimals

- ✓ Rounding Decimals

- ✓ Adding and Subtracting Decimals

- ✓ Multiplying and Dividing Decimals

*"Do not worry about your difficulties in mathematics. I can assure you mine are still greater." ~ Albert Einstein*

# Comparing Decimals

**Step-by-step guide:**

Decimals: is a fraction written in a special form. For example, instead of writing $\frac{1}{2}$ you can write 0.5.

For comparing decimals:

✓ Compare each digit of two decimals in the same place value.
✓ Start from left. Compare hundreds, tens, ones, tenth, hundredth, etc.
✓ To compare numbers, use these symbols:
- Equal to =,        Less than <,       Greater than >
  Greater than or equal ≥,    Less than or equal ≤

**Examples:**

1) Compare **0.20** and **0.02**.

   0.20 is greater than 0.02, because the tenth place of 0.20 is 2, but the tenth place of 0.02 is zero. Then: 0.20 > 0.02

2) Compare **0.0210** and **0.110**.

   0.0.110 is greater than 0.0210, because the tenth place of 0.110 is 1, but the tenth place of 0.0210 is zero. Then: 0.0210 < 0.110

✎ *Write the correct comparison symbol (>, < or =).*

1)  0.50 ☐ 0.050

2) 0.025 ☐ 0.25

3) 2.060 ☐ 2.07

4) 1.75 ☐ 1.07

5) 4.04 ☐ 0.440

6) 3.05 ☐ 3.5

7) 5.05 ☐ 5.050

8) 1.02 ☐ 1.1

9) 2.45 ☐ 2.125

10) 0.932 ☐ 0.0932

11) 3.15 ☐ 3.150

12) 0.718 ☐ 0.89

# Rounding Decimals

**Step-by-step guide:**

- ✓ We can round decimals to a certain accuracy or number of decimal places. This is used to make calculation easier to do and results easier to understand, when exact values are not too important.
- ✓ First, you'll need to remember your place values: For example:

## 12.4567

| 1: tens | 2: ones | 4: tenths |
|---------|---------|-----------|
| 5: hundredths | 6: thousandths | 7: tens thousandths |

- ✓ To round a decimal, find the place value you'll round to.
- ✓ Find the digit to the right of the place value you're rounding to. If it is **5** or bigger, add **1** to the place value you're rounding to and remove all digits on its right side. If the digit to the right of the place value is less than **5**, keep the place value and remove all digits on the right.

**Examples:**

1) Round 2.1837 to the thousandth place value.

First look at the next place value to the right, (tens thousandths). It's 7 and it is greater than 5. Thus add 1 to the digit in the thousandth place.

Thousandth place is 3. → 3 + 1 = 4, then, the answer is 2.184

2) 2.1837 rounded to the nearest hundredth.

First look at the next place value to the right of thousandths. It's 3 and it is less than 5, thus remove all the digits to the right. Then, the answer is 2.18.

✍ *Round each decimal to the nearest whole number.*

| | | |
|---|---|---|
| 1) 23.18 | 3) 14.45 | 5) 3.95 |
| 2) 8.6 | 4) 7.5 | 6) 56.7 |

✍ *Round each decimal to the nearest tenth.*

| | | |
|---|---|---|
| 7) 22.652 | 9) 47.847 | 11) 16.184 |
| 8) 30.342 | 10) 82.88 | 12) 71.79 |

# Adding and Subtracting Decimals

**Step-by-step guide:**

- ✓ Line up the numbers.

- ✓ Add zeros to have same number of digits for both numbers if necessary.

- ✓ Add or subtract using column addition or subtraction.

**Examples:**

1) Add. $2.5 + 1.24 =$

First line up the numbers: $\begin{array}{r} 2.5 \\ + 1.24 \\ \hline \end{array}$ → Add zeros to have same number of digits for both

numbers. $\begin{array}{r} 2.50 \\ + 1.24 \\ \hline \end{array}$ , Start with the hundredths place. $0 + 4 = 4$, $\begin{array}{r} 2.50 \\ + 1.24 \\ \hline 4 \end{array}$ , Continue with tenths

place. $5 + 2 = 7$, $\begin{array}{r} 2.50 \\ + 1.24 \\ \hline .74 \end{array}$ . Add the ones place. $2 + 1 = 3$, $\begin{array}{r} 2.50 \\ + 1.24 \\ \hline 3.74 \end{array}$

2) Subtract decimals. $4.67 + 2.15 = \begin{array}{r} 4.67 \\ - 2.15 \\ \hline \end{array}$

Start with the hundredths place. $7 - 5 = 2$, $\begin{array}{r} 4.67 \\ - 2.15 \\ \hline 2 \end{array}$ , continue with tenths place. $6 - 1 = 5$

$\begin{array}{r} 4.67 \\ - 2.15 \\ \hline .52 \end{array}$ , subtract the ones place. $4 - 2 = 2$, $\begin{array}{r} 4.67 \\ - 2.15 \\ \hline 2.52 \end{array}$ .

✎ *Find the sum or difference.*

1) $31.13 - 11.45 =$

2) $35.25 + 24.47 =$

3) $73.50 + 22.78 =$

4) $56.67 - 44.39 =$

5) $71.47 + 16.25 =$

6) $68.99 - 53.61 =$

7) $66.24 - 23.11 =$

8) $39.75 + 12.85 =$

# Multiplying and Dividing Decimals

**Step-by-step guide:**

For Multiplication:

✓ Ignore the decimal point and set up and multiply the numbers as you do with whole numbers.
Count the total number of decimal places in both of the factors.
Place the decimal point in the product.
For Division:

✓ If the divisor is not a whole number, move decimal point to right to make it a whole number. Do the same for dividend.
✓ Divide similar to whole numbers.

**Examples:**

1) Find the product. $0.50 \times 0.20 =$

Set up and multiply the numbers as you do with whole numbers. Line up the numbers: $\frac{50}{\times 20}$, Start with

the ones place $\rightarrow 50 \times 0 = 0$, $\frac{50}{\times 20} \over 0$, Continue with other digits $\rightarrow 50 \times 2 = 100$, $\frac{50}{\times 20} \over 1,000$, Count the

total number of decimal places in both of the factors. (4). Then Place the decimal point in the product.

Then: $\frac{0.50}{\times 0.20} \over 0.1000$ $\rightarrow 0.50 \times 0.20 = 0.1$

2) Find the quotient. $1.20 \div 0.2 =$

The divisor is not a whole number. Multiply it by 10 to get 2. Do the same for the dividend to get 12.
Now, divide: $12 \div 2 = 6$. The answer is 6.

✍ *Find the product and quotient.*

1) $0.5 \times 0.4 =$      5) $1.92 \times 0.8 =$      9) $4.2 \div 2 =$

2) $2.5 \times 0.2 =$      6) $0.55 \times 0.4 =$      10) $8.6 \div 0.5 =$

3) $1.25 \times 0.5 =$      7) $1.67 \div 100 =$      11) $12.6 \div 0.2 =$

4) $0.75 \times 0.2 =$      8) $52.2 \div 1,000 =$      12) $16.5 \div 5 =$

# Answers – Day 4

## *Comparing Decimals*

1) >
2) <
3) <
4) >
5) >
6) <

7) =
8) <
9) >
10) >
11) =
12) <

## *Rounding Decimals*

1) 23
2) 9
3) 14
4) 8

5) 4
6) 57
7) 22.7
8) 30.3

9) 47.8
10) 82.9
11) 16.2
12) 71.8

## *Adding and Subtracting Decimals*

1) 19.68
2) 59.72
3) 96.28

4) 12.28
5) 87.72
6) 15.38

7) 43.13
8) 52.60

## *Multiplying and Dividing Decimals*

1) 0.20
2) 0.50
3) 0.625
4) 0.15

5) 1.536
6) 0.22
7) 0.0167
8) 0.0522

9) 2.10
10) 17.2
11) 63
12) 3.3

# Day 5: Factoring Numbers

## Math Topics that you'll learn today:

- ✓ Factoring Numbers

- ✓ Greatest Common Factor

- ✓ Least Common Multiple

*"The study of mathematics, like the Nile, begins in minuteness but ends in magnificence."*

*~ Charles Caleb Colton*

# Factoring Numbers

**Step-by-step guide:**

✓ Factoring numbers means to break the numbers into their prime factors.
✓ First few prime numbers: $2, 3, 5, 7, 11, 13, 17, 19$

**Examples:**

1) List all positive factors of **12**.

Write the upside-down division:
The second column is the answer.
Then: $12 = 2 \times 2 \times 3$ or $12 = 2^2 \times 3$

$$
\begin{array}{c|c}
12 & 2 \\
\hline
6 & 2 \\
\hline
3 & 3 \\
\hline
1 &
\end{array}
$$

2) List all positive factors of **20**.

Write the upside-down division:
The second column is the answer.
Then: $20 = 2 \times 2 \times 5$ or $20 = 2^2 \times 5$

$$
\begin{array}{c|c}
20 & 2 \\
\hline
10 & 2 \\
\hline
5 & 5 \\
\hline
1 &
\end{array}
$$

✎ *List all positive factors of each number.*

| | | |
|---|---|---|
| 1) 8 | 5) 25 | 9) 42 |
| 2) 9 | 6) 28 | 10) 48 |
| 3) 15 | 7) 26 | 11) 50 |
| 4) 16 | 8) 35 | 12) 36 |

# Greatest Common Factor

**Step-by-step guide:**

- ✓ List the prime factors of each number.
- ✓ Multiply common prime factors.
- ✓ If there are no common prime factors, the GCF is **1**.

**Examples:**

1) Find the GCF for **10** and **15**.

The factors of 10 are: $\{1, 2, 5, 10\}$

The factors of 15 are: $\{1, 3, 5, 15\}$

There is 5 in common,

Then the greatest common factor is: 5.

2) Find the GCF for **8** and **20**.

The factors of 8 are: $\{1, 2, 4, 8\}$

The factors of 20 are: $\{1, 2, 4, 5, 10, 20\}$

There is 2 and 4 in common.

Then the greatest common factor is: $2 \times 4 = 8$.

✎ *Find the GCF for each number pair.*

1) $4, 2$               5) $5, 10$              9) $5, 12$

2) $3, 5$               6) $6, 12$              10) $4, 14$

3) $2, 6$               7) $7, 14$              11) $15, 18$

4) $4, 7$               8) $6, 14$              12) $12, 20$

# Least Common Multiple

**Step-by-step guide:**

- ✓ Least Common Multiple is the smallest multiple that 2 or more numbers have in common.
- ✓ How to find LCM: list out all the multiples of each number and then find the first one they have in common.

**Examples:**

1) Find the LCM for **3** and **4**.

Multiples of 3: $3, 6, 9, 12, 15, 18, 21, 24$

Multiples of 4: $4, 8, 12, 16, 20, 24$

$LCM = 12$

2) Find the LCM for **9** and **12**.

Multiples of 9: $9, 18, 27, 36, 45$

Multiples of 12: $12, 24, 36, 48$

$LCM = 36$

✍ *Find the LCM for each number pair.*

| | | |
|---|---|---|
| 1) $3, 6$ | 5) $6, 18$ | 9) $4, 18$ |
| 2) $5, 10$ | 6) $10, 12$ | 10) $9, 12$ |
| 3) $6, 14$ | 7) $4, 12$ | 11) $12, 16$ |
| 4) $8, 9$ | 8) $5, 15$ | 12) $15, 18$ |

# Answers – Day 5

## Factoring Numbers

1) 1, 2, 4, 8

2) 1, 3, 9

3) 1, 3, 5, 15

4) 1, 2, 4, 8, 16

5) 1, 5, 25

6) 1, 2, 4, 7, 14, 28

7) 1, 2, 13, 26

8) 1, 5, 7, 35

9) 1, 2, 3, 6, 7, 14, 21, 42

10) 1, 2, 3, 4, 6, 8, 12, 16, 24, 48

11) 1, 2, 5, 10, 25, 50

12) 1, 2, 3, 4, 6, 9, 12, 18, 36

## Greatest Common Factor

1) 2

2) 1

3) 2

4) 1

5) 5

6) 6

7) 7

8) 2

9) 1

10) 2

11) 3

12) 4

## Least Common Multiple

1) 6

2) 10

3) 42

4) 72

5) 18

6) 60

7) 12

8) 15

9) 36

10) 36

11) 48

12) 90

# Day 6: Integers

## Math Topics that you'll learn today:

- ✓ Adding and Subtracting Integers

- ✓ Multiplying and Dividing Integers

- ✓ Ordering Integers and Numbers

*"Without mathematics, there's nothing you can do. Everything around you is mathematics. Everything around you is numbers." – Shakuntala Devi*

# Adding and Subtracting Integers

**Step-by-step guide:**

✓ Integers includes: zero, counting numbers, and the negative of the counting numbers. $\{..., -3, -2, -1, 0, 1, 2, 3, ...\}$
✓ Add a positive integer by moving to the right on the number line.
✓ Add a negative integer by moving to the left on the number line.
✓ Subtract an integer by adding its opposite.

**Examples:**

1) Solve. $(-8) - (-5) =$

Keep the first number, and convert the sign of the second number to it's opposite. (change subtraction into addition. Then: $(-8) + 5 = -3$

2) Solve. $10 + (4 - 8) =$

First subtract the numbers in brackets, $4 - 8 = -4$

Then: $10 + (-4) = \rightarrow$ change addition into subtraction: $10 - 4 = 6$

✎ *Find each sum or difference.*

1) $12 + (-5) =$

2) $(-14) + (-18) =$

3) $8 + (-28) =$

4) $43 + (-12) =$

5) $(-7) + (-11) + 4 =$

6) $37 + (-16) + 12 =$

7) $(-12) - (-8) =$

8) $15 - (-20) =$

9) $(-11) - 25 =$

10) $30 - (-16) =$

11) $56 - (45 - 23) =$

12) $15 - (-4) - (-34) =$

# Multiplying and Dividing Integers

**Step-by-step guide:**

Use these rules for multiplying and dividing integers:
- ✓ (negative) × (negative) = positive
- ✓ (negative) ÷ (negative) = positive
- ✓ (negative) × (positive) = negative
- ✓ (negative) ÷ (positive) = negative
- ✓ (positive) × (positive) = positive

**Examples:**

1) Solve. $(2 - 5) \times (3) =$

First subtract the numbers in brackets, $2 - 5 = -3 \rightarrow (-3) \times (3) =$

Now use this formula: (negative) × (positive) = negative
$(-3) \times (3) = -9$

2) Solve. $(-12) + (48 \div 6) =$

First divided 48 by 6 , the numbers in brackets, $48 \div 6 = 8$

$(-12) + (8) = -12 + 8 = -4$

✎ *Find each product or quotient.*

1) $(-7) \times (-8) =$

2) $(-4) \times 5 =$

3) $5 \times (-11) =$

4) $(-5) \times (-20) =$

5) $-(2) \times (-8) \times 3 =$

6) $(12 - 4) \times (-10) =$

7) $16 \div (-4) =$

8) $(-25) \div (-5) =$

9) $(-40) \div (-8) =$

10) $64 \div (-8) =$

11) $(-49) \div 7 =$

12) $(-112) \div (-4) =$

# Ordering Integers and Numbers

**Step-by-step guide:**

✓ When using a number line, numbers increase as you move to the right.
✓ When comparing two numbers, think about their position on number line. If one number is on the right side of another number, it is a bigger number. For example, $-3$ is bigger than $-5$ because it is on the right side of $-5$ on number line.

**Examples:**

1) Order this set of integers from least to greatest. $-2, 1, -5, -1, 2, 4$
   The smallest number is $-5$ and the largest number is $4$.

   Now compare the integers and order them from greatest to least:
   $-5 < -2 < -1 < 1 < 2 < 4$

2) Order each set of integers from greatest to least. $10, -6, -2, 5, -8, 4$
   The largest number is $10$ and the smallest number is $-8$.

   Now compare the integers and order them from least to greatest:
   $10 > 5 > 4 > -2 > -6 > -8$

✍ *Order each set of integers from least to greatest.*

1) $7, -9, -6, -1, 3$      ___, ___, ___, ___, ___, ___
2) $-4, -11, 5, 12, 9$      ___, ___, ___, ___, ___, ___
3) $18, -12, -19, 21, -20$      ___, ___, ___, ___, ___, ___
4) $-15, -25, 18, -7, 32$      ___, ___, ___, ___, ___, ___

✍ *Order each set of integers from greatest to least.*

5) $11, 16, -9, -12, -4$      ___, ___, ___, ___, ___, ___
6) $23, 31, -14, -20, 39$      ___, ___, ___, ___, ___, ___
7) $45, -21, -18, 55, -5$      ___, ___, ___, ___, ___, ___
8) $68, 81, -14, -10, 94$      ___, ___, ___, ___, ___, ___

# Answers – Day 6

### Adding and Subtracting Integers

1) 7

2) −32

3) −20

4) 31

5) −14

6) 33

7) −4

8) 35

9) −36

10) 46

11) 34

12) 53

### Multiplying and Dividing Integers

1) 56

2) −20

3) −55

4) 100

5) 48

6) −80

7) −4

8) 5

9) 5

10) −8

11) −7

12) 28

### Ordering Integers and Numbers

1) $-9, -6, -1, 3, 7$

2) $-11, -4, 5, 9, 12$

3) $-20, -19, -12, 18, 21$

4) $-25, -15, -7, 18, 32$

5) $16, 11, -4, -9, -12$

6) $39, 31, 23, -14, -20$

7) $55, 45, -5, -18, -21$

8) $94, 81, 68, -10, -14$

# Day 7: Order of Operations

**Math Topics that you'll learn today:**

- ✓ Order of Operations

- ✓ Integers and Absolute Value

*"Sometimes the questions are complicated and the answers are simple." - Dr. Seuss*

# Order of Operations

**Step-by-step guide:**

When there is more than one math operation, use PEMDAS:

✓ Parentheses

✓ Exponents

✓ Multiplication and Division (from left to right)

✓ Addition and Subtraction (from left to right)

**Examples:**

1) Solve. $(5 + 7) \div (3^2 \div 3) =$

First simplify inside parentheses: $(12) \div (9 \div 3) = (12) \div (3) =$
Then: $(12) \div (3) = 4$

2) Solve. $(11 \times 5) - (12 - 7) =$

First simplify inside parentheses: $(11 \times 5) - (12 - 7) = (55) - (5) =$

Then: $(55) - (5) = 50$

✍ *Evaluate each expression.*

1) $5 + (4 \times 2) =$

2) $13 - (2 \times 5) =$

3) $(16 \times 2) + 18 =$

4) $(12 - 5) - (4 \times 3) =$

5) $25 + (14 \div 2) =$

6) $(18 \times 5) \div 5 =$

7) $(48 \div 2) \times (-4) =$

8) $(7 \times 5) + (25 - 12) =$

9) $64 + (3 \times 2) + 8 =$

10) $(20 \times 5) \div (4 + 1) =$

11) $(-9) + (12 \times 6) + 15 =$

12) $(7 \times 8) - (56 \div 4) =$

# Integers and Absolute Value

**Step-by-step guide:**

✓ To find an absolute value of a number, just find its distance from **0** on number line! For example, the distance of **12** and **−12** from zero on number line is **12**!

**Examples:**

1) Solve. $\frac{|-18|}{9} \times |5 - 8| =$

First find $|-18|$, →the absolute value of $-18$ is 18, then: $|-18| = 18$

$\frac{18}{9} \times |5 - 8| =$

Next, solve $|5 - 8|$, → $|5 - 8| = |-3|$, the absolute value of $-3$ is 3. $|-3| = 3$

Then: $\frac{18}{9} \times 3 = 2 \times 3 = 6$

2) Solve. $|10 - 5| \times \frac{|-2\times6|}{3} =$

First solve $|10 - 5|$, → $|10 - 5| = |5|$, the absolute value of 5 is 5, $|5| = 5$

$5 \times \frac{|-2\times6|}{3} =$

Now solve $|-2 \times 6|$, → $|-2 \times 6| = |-12|$, the absolute value of $-12$ is 12, $|-12| = 12$

Then: $5 \times \frac{12}{3} = 5 \times 4 = 20$

## ✍ *Evaluate the value.*

1) $8 - |2 - 14| - |-2| =$

2) $|-2| - \frac{|-10|}{2} =$

3) $\frac{|-36|}{6} \times |-6| =$

4) $\frac{|5 \times -3|}{5} \times \frac{|-20|}{4} =$

5) $|2 \times -4| + \frac{|-40|}{5} =$

6) $\frac{|-28|}{4} \times \frac{|-55|}{11} =$

7) $|-12 + 4| \times \frac{|-4\times5|}{2} =$

8) $\frac{|-10 \times 3|}{2} \times |-12| =$

# Answers – Day 7

## Order of Operations

1) 13
2) 3
3) 50
4) −5
5) 32
6) 18

7) −96
8) 48
9) 78
10) 20
11) 78
12) 42

## Integers and Absolute Value

1) −6
2) −3
3) 36
4) 15

5) 16
6) 35
7) 80
8) 180

# Day 8: Ratios

**Math Topics that you'll learn today:**

- ✓ Simplifying Ratios

- ✓ Proportional Ratios

*Mathematics is the door and key to the sciences. — Roger Bacon*

# Simplifying Ratios

**Step-by-step guide:**

- ✓ Ratios are used to make comparisons between two numbers.
- ✓ Ratios can be written as a fraction, using the word "to", or with a colon.
- ✓ You can calculate equivalent ratios by multiplying or dividing both sides of the ratio by the same number.

**Examples:**

1) Simplify. $8:4 =$

Both numbers 8 and 4 are divisible by 4 , $\Rightarrow 8 \div 4 = 2, 4 \div 4 = 1,$

Then: $8:4 = 2:1$

2) Simplify. $\dfrac{12}{36} =$

Both numbers 12 and 36 are divisible by 12, $\Rightarrow 12 \div 12 = 1, 36 \div 12 = 3,$

Then: $\dfrac{12}{36} = \dfrac{1}{3}$

✍ *Reduce each ratio.*

1) $12:8 = $ ___ : ___

2) $2:20 = $ ___ : ___

3) $3:36 = $ ___ : ___

4) $8:16 = $ ___ : ___

5) $6:100 = $ ___ : ___

6) $10:60 = $ ___ : ___

7) $21:49 = $ ___ : ___

8) $20:40 = $ ___ : ___

9) $10:50 = $ ___ : ___

10) $14:18 = $ ___ : ___

11) $45:27 = $ ___ : ___

12) $49:21 = $ ___ : ___

# Proportional Ratios

**Step-by-step guide:**

✓ A proportion means that two ratios are equal. It can be written in two ways:
$$\frac{a}{b} = \frac{c}{d}, \quad a : b = c : d$$

✓ The proportion $\frac{a}{b} = \frac{c}{d}$ can be written as: $a \times d = c \times b$

**Examples:**

1) Solve this proportion for $x$. $\frac{4}{8} = \frac{5}{x}$

Use cross multiplication: $\frac{4}{8} = \frac{5}{x} \Rightarrow 4 \times x = 5 \times 8 \Rightarrow 4x = 40$

Divide to find $x$: $x = \frac{40}{4} \Rightarrow x = 10$

2) If a box contains red and blue balls in ratio of $2 : 3$ red to blue, how many red balls are there if **90** blue balls are in the box?

Write a proportion and solve. $\frac{2}{3} = \frac{x}{90}$

Use cross multiplication: $2 \times 90 = 3 \times x \Rightarrow 180 = 3x$

Divide to find $x$: $x = \frac{180}{3} \Rightarrow x = 60$

✏️ *Solve each proportion.*

1) $\frac{2}{5} = \frac{14}{x}, x =$ _____

2) $\frac{1}{6} = \frac{7}{x}, x =$ _____

3) $\frac{3}{5} = \frac{27}{x}, x =$ _____

4) $\frac{1}{5} = \frac{x}{80}, x =$ _____

5) $\frac{3}{7} = \frac{x}{63}, x =$ _____

6) $\frac{1}{4} = \frac{13}{x}, x =$ _____

7) $\frac{7}{9} = \frac{56}{x}, x =$ _____

8) $\frac{6}{11} = \frac{42}{x}, x =$ _____

9) $\frac{4}{7} = \frac{x}{77}, x =$ _____

10) $\frac{5}{13} = \frac{x}{143}, x =$ _____

11) $\frac{7}{19} = \frac{x}{209}, x =$ _____

12) $\frac{3}{13} = \frac{x}{195}, x =$ _____

# Answers – Day 8

## Simplifying Ratios

1)  $3:2$
2)  $1:10$
3)  $1:12$
4)  $1:2$
5)  $3:50$
6)  $1:6$

7)  $3:7$
8)  $1:2$
9)  $1:5$
10) $7:9$
11) $5:3$
12) $7:3$

## Proportional Ratios

1)  35
2)  42
3)  45
4)  16
5)  27
6)  52

7)  72
8)  77
9)  44
10) 55
11) 77
12) 45

# Day 9: Similarity and Proportions

**Math Topics that you'll learn today:**

✓ Create a Proportion

✓ Similarity and Ratios

✓ Simple Interest

*Mathematics - the unshaken Foundation of Sciences, and the plentiful Fountain of Advantage to human affairs. –*

*Isaac Barrow*

# Create a Proportion

**Step-by-step guide:**

   ✓ A proportion contains two equal fractions! A proportion simply means that two fractions are equal.

   ✓ To create a proportion, simply find (or create) two equal fractions.

**Examples:**

1) Express ratios as a Proportion.
**120 miles on 4 gallons of gas, how many miles on 1 gallon of gas?**

First create a fraction: $\frac{120 \ miles}{4 \ gallons}$ , and divide: $120 \div 4 = 30$

Then: 30 miles per gallon

2) State if this pair of ratios form a proportion. $\frac{3}{5}$ and $\frac{24}{45}$

Use cross multiplication: $\frac{3}{5} = \frac{24}{45} \rightarrow 3 \times 45 = 5 \times 24 \rightarrow 135 = 120$, which is not correct.

Therefore, this pair of ratios doesn't form a proportion.

✍ *State if each pair of ratios form a proportion.*

1) $\frac{3}{10}$ and $\frac{9}{30}$          5) $\frac{2}{5}$ and $\frac{16}{45}$          9) $\frac{6}{17}$ and $\frac{36}{85}$

2) $\frac{1}{2}$ and $\frac{16}{32}$          6) $\frac{4}{9}$ and $\frac{40}{81}$          10) $\frac{2}{7}$ and $\frac{24}{86}$

3) $\frac{5}{6}$ and $\frac{35}{42}$          7) $\frac{6}{11}$ and $\frac{42}{77}$          11) $\frac{12}{19}$ and $\frac{156}{247}$

4) $\frac{3}{7}$ and $\frac{27}{72}$          8) $\frac{1}{6}$ and $\frac{8}{48}$          12) $\frac{13}{21}$ and $\frac{182}{294}$

# Similarity and Ratios

**Step-by-step guide:**

✓ Two or more figures are similar if the corresponding angles are equal, and the corresponding sides are in proportion.

**Examples:**

1) A girl **160 cm** tall, stands **360 cm** from a lamp post at night. Her shadow from the light is **90 cm** long. How high is the lamp post?

Write the proportion and solve for missing side.

$$\frac{Smaller\ triangle\ height}{Smaller\ triangle\ base} = \frac{Bigger\ triangle\ height}{Bigger\ triangle\ base}$$

$$\Rightarrow \frac{90cm}{160cm} = \frac{90+360cm}{x} \Rightarrow 90x = 160 \times 450 \Rightarrow x = 800\ cm$$

160 cm

90 cm          360 cm

2) A tree **32 feet** tall casts a shadow **12 feet** long. Jack is **6 feet** tall. How long is Jack's shadow?

Write a proportion and solve for the missing number.

$$\frac{32}{12} = \frac{6}{x} \rightarrow 32x = 6 \times 12$$

$$32x = 72 \rightarrow x = \frac{72}{32} = 2.25$$

✎ *Solve.*

1) Two rectangles are similar. The first is 6 feet wide and 20 feet long. The second is 15 feet wide. What is the length of the second rectangle? _____

**2)** Two rectangles are similar. One is 2.5 meters by 9 meters. The longer side of the second rectangle is 22.5 meters. What is the other side of the second rectangle? _____

3) A building casts a shadow 24 *ft* long. At the same time a girl 5 *ft* tall casts a shadow 2 *ft* long. How tall is the building? _____

4) The scale of a map of Texas is 2 inches: 45 miles. If you measure the distance from Dallas to Martin County as 14.4 inches, approximately how far is Martin County from Dallas? _____

# Simple Interest

### Step-by-step guide:

✓ Simple Interest: The charge for borrowing money or the return for lending it. To solve a simple interest problem, use this formula:

Interest = principal × rate × time  ⇒  $I = p \times r \times t$

### Examples:

1) Find simple interest for **$450** investment at **7%** for **8** years.

Use Interest formula: $I = prt$

$p = \$450, \text{r} = 7\% = \dfrac{7}{100} = 0.07$ and $t = 8$

Then: $I = 450 \times 0.07 \times 8 = \$252$

2) Find simple interest for **$5,200** at **4%** for **3** years.

Use Interest formula: $I = prt$

$p = \$5,200, \text{r} = 4\% = \dfrac{4}{100} = 0.04$ and $t = 3$

Then: $I = 5,200 \times 0.04 \times 3 = \$624$

✎ *Determine the simple interest for these loans.*

1) $1,300 at 5% for 6 years.      $ _____

2) $5,400 at 3.5% for 6 months.      $ _____

3) $600 at 4% for 9 months.      $ _____

4) $24,000 at 5.5% for 5 years.      $ _____

5) $15,600 at 3% for 2 years.      $ _____

6) $1,200 at 5.5% for 4 years.      $ _____

7) $1,600 at 4.5% for 9 months.      $ _____

8) $12,000 at 2.2% for 5 years.      $ _____

# Answers – Day 9

## Create a Proportion

1) Yes

2) Yes

3) Yes

4) No

5) No

6) No

7) Yes

8) Yes

9) No

10) No

11) Yes

12) Yes

## Similarity and ratios

1) 50 *feet*

2) 6.25 *meters*

3) 60 *feet*

4) 324 *miles*

## Simple Interest

1) $390.00

2) $94.50

3) $18.00

4) $6,600.00

5) $936.00

6) $264.00

7) $54

8) $1,320.00

# Day 10: Percentage

## Math Topics that you'll learn today:

✓ Percentage Calculations

✓ Percent Problems

*Mathematics is no more computation than typing is literature.*

*- John Allen Paulos*

# Percentage Calculations

Step-by-step guide:

- ✓ Percent is a ratio of a number and **100**. It always has the same denominator, 100. Percent symbol is %.
- ✓ Percent is another way to write decimals or fractions. For example:

$$40\% = 0.40 = \frac{40}{100} = \frac{2}{5}$$

- ✓ Use the following formula to find part, whole, or percent:

$$part = \frac{percent}{100} \times whole$$

Examples:

1) What is **10%** of 45? Use the following formula: $part = \frac{percent}{100} \times whole$

$$part = \frac{10}{100} \times 45 \rightarrow part = \frac{1}{10} \times 45 \rightarrow part = \frac{45}{10} \rightarrow part = 4.5$$

2) What is **15%** of 24? Use the percent formula: $part = \frac{percent}{100} \times whole$

$$part = \frac{15}{100} \times 24 \rightarrow part = \frac{360}{100} \rightarrow part = 3.6$$

✎ *Calculate the given percent of each value.*

1) 2% of 50 = ____

2) 10% of 30 = ____

3) 20% of 25 = ____

4) 50% of 80 = ____

5) 40% of 200 = ____

6) 20% of 45 = ____

7) 35% of 20 = ____

8) 12% of 400 = ____

9) 40% of 90 = ____

10) 25% of 812 = ____

11) 32% of 600 = ____

12) 87% of 500 = ____

## Percent Problems

**Step-by-step guide:**

- ✓ In each percent problem, we are looking for the base, or part or the percent.
- ✓ Use the following equations to find each missing section.
  - ○ Base = Part ÷ Percent
  - ○ Part = Percent × Base
  - ○ Percent = Part ÷ Base

**Examples:**

1) **1.2 is what percent of 24?**

   In this problem, we are looking for the percent. Use the following equation:
   $$Percent = Part \div Base \rightarrow Percent = 1.2 \div 24 = 0.05 = 5\%$$

2) **20 is 5% of what number?**

   Use the following formula: $Base = Part \div Percent \rightarrow Base = 20 \div 0.05 = 400$
   20 is 5% of 400.

✎ *Solve each problem.*

1) 20 is what percent of 50? ____%

2) 18 is what percent of 90? ____%

3) 12 is what percent of 15? ____%

4) 16 is what percent of 200? ____%

5) 24 is what percent of 800? ____%

6) 48 is what percent of 400? ____%

7) 90 is 12 percent of what number? ____

8) 24 is 8 percent of what? ____

9) 60 is 15 percent of what number? ____

10) 42 *is 12 percent of what?* ___

11) 11 *is 25 percent of what?* ___

12) 8 *is 12.5 percent of what?* ___

# Answers – Day 10

## *Percentage Calculations*

1)  1

2)  3

3)  5

4)  40

5)  80

6)  9

7)  7

8)  48

9)  36

10) 203

11) 192

12) 435

## *Percent Problems*

1) 40%

2) 20%

3) 80%

4) 8%

5) 3%

6) 12%

7) 750

8) 300

9) 400

10) 350

11) 44

12) 64

# Day 11: Percent of Change

**Math Topics that you'll learn today:**

✓ Percent of Increase and Decrease

✓ Discount, Tax and Tip

*Mathematics is a great motivator for all humans. Because its career starts with zero and it never end (infinity).*

# Percent of Increase and Decrease

**Step-by-step guide:**

To find the percentage of increase or decrease:
✓ New Number – Original Number
✓ The result ÷ Original Number × 100
✓ If your answer is a negative number, then this is a percentage decrease. If it is positive, then this is a percent of increase.

**Examples:**

1) Increased by **50**%, the numbers **84** becomes:

First find 50% of 84 → $\frac{50}{100} \times 84 = \frac{50 \times 84}{100} = 42$

Then: $84 + 42 = 126$

2) The price of a shirt increases from **$10** to **$14**. What is the percent increase?
First: $14 - 10 = 4$
4 is the result. Then: $4 \div 10 = \frac{4}{10} = 0.4 = 40\%$

✎ *Solve each percent of change word problem.*

1) Bob got a raise, and his hourly wage increased from $12 to $15. What is the percent increase? _____ %

2) The price of a pair of shoes increases from $20 to $32. What is the percent increase? _____ %

3) At a coffeeshop, the price of a cup of coffee increased from $1.20 to $1.44. What is the percent increase in the cost of the coffee? _____ %

4) 6 *cm* are cut from a 24 *cm* board. What is the percent decrease in length? _____ %

5) In a class, the number of students has been increased from 18 to 27. What is the percent increase? _____ %

6) The price of gasoline rose from $2.40 to $2.76 in one month. By what percent did the gas price rise? _____ %

7) A shirt was originally priced at $48. It went on sale for $38.40. What was the percent that the shirt was discounted? _____ %

# Discount, Tax and Tip

**Step-by-step guide:**

- ✓ Discount = Multiply the regular price by the rate of discount
- ✓ Selling price = original price – discount
- ✓ Tax: To find tax, multiply the tax rate to the taxable amount (income, property value, etc.)
- ✓ To find tip, multiply the rate to the selling price.

**Examples:**

1) With an **10**% discount, Ella was able to save $**20** on a dress. What was the original price of the dress?

$10\% \ of \ x = \ 20, \frac{10}{100} \times x = \ 20, x = \frac{100 \times 20}{10} = 200$

2) Sophia purchased a sofa for $**530.40**. The sofa is regularly priced at $**624**. What was the percent discount Sophia received on the sofa?

Use this formula: $percent = Part \div base = 530.40 \div 624 = 0.85 = 85\%$
Therefore, the discount is: $100\% - 85\% = 15\%$

✎ *Find the selling price of each item.*

1) Original price of a computer: $500

   Tax: 6%, Selling price: $_____

2) Original price of a laptop: $350

   Tax: 8%, Selling price: $_____

3) Original price of a sofa: $800

   Tax: 7%, Selling price: $_____

4) Original price of a car: $18,500

   Tax: 8.5%, Selling price: $_____

5) Original price of a Table: $250

   Tax: 5%, Selling price: $_____

6) Original price of a house: $250,000

   Tax: 6.5%  Selling price: $_____

7) Original price of a tablet: $400

   Discount: 20%, Selling price: $_____

8) Original price of a chair: $150

   Discount: 15%, Selling price: $_____

9) Original price of a book: $50

   Discount: 25%, Selling price: $_____

10) Original price of a cellphone: $500

   Discount: 10%, Selling price: $_____

# Answers – Day 11

### Percent of Increase and Decrease

1) 25%

2) 60%

3) 20%

4) 25%

5) 50%

6) 15%

7) 20%

### Markup, Discount, and Tip

1) $530.00

2) $378.00

3) $856.00

4) $20,072.50

5) $262.50

6) $266,250

7) $320.00

8) $127.50

9) $37.50

10) $450.00

# Day 12: Exponents and Variables

## Math Topics that you'll learn today:

- ✓ Multiplication Property of Exponents

- ✓ Division Property of Exponents

- ✓ Powers of Products and Quotients

*Mathematics is an art of human understanding. — William Thurston*

# Multiplication Property of Exponents

**Step-by-step guide:**

✓ Exponents are shorthand for repeated multiplication of the same number by itself. For example, instead of $2 \times 2$, we can write $2^2$. For $3 \times 3 \times 3 \times 3$, we can write $3^4$

✓ In algebra, a variable is a letter used to stand for a number. The most common letters are: $x, y, z, a, b, c, m,$ and $n$.

✓ Exponent's rules: $x^a \times x^b = x^{a+b}$ , $\frac{x^a}{x^b} = x^{a-b}$

$$(x^a)^b = x^{a \times b}, \qquad (xy)^a = x^a \times y^a , (\frac{a}{b})^c = \frac{a^c}{b^c}$$

**Examples:**

1) Multiply. $-2x^5 \times 7x^3 =$

Use Exponent's rules: $x^a \times x^b = x^{a+b} \rightarrow x^5 \times x^3 = x^{5+3} = x^8$

Then: $-2x^5 \times 7x^3 = -14x^8$

2) Multiply. $(x^2 y^4)^3 =$

Use Exponent's rules: $(x^a)^b = x^{a \times b}$. Then: $(x^2 y^4)^3 = x^{2 \times 3} y^{4 \times 3} = x^6 y^{12}$

✎ ***Simplify and write the answer in exponential form.***

1) $x^4 \times 3x =$

2) $x \times 2x^2 =$

3) $5x^4 \times 5x^4 =$

4) $2yx^2 \times 2x =$

5) $3x^4 \times y^2 x^4 =$

6) $y^2 x^3 \times y^5 x^2 =$

7) $4yx^3 \times 2x^2 y^3 =$

8) $6x^2 \times 6x^3 y^4 =$

9) $3x^4 y^5 \times 7x^2 y^3 =$

10) $7x^2 y^5 \times 9xy^3 =$

11) $7xy^4 \times 4x^3 y^3 =$

12) $3x^5 y^3 \times 8x^2 y^3 =$

# Division Property of Exponents

## Step-by-step guide:

✓ For division of exponents use these formulas: $\frac{x^a}{x^b} = x^{a-b}$ , $x \neq 0$

$$\frac{x^a}{x^b} = \frac{1}{x^{b-a}} , x \neq 0, \qquad \frac{1}{x^b} = x^{-b}$$

## *Examples:*

1) Simplify. $\frac{4x^3y}{36x^2y^3} =$

First cancel the common factor: $4 \rightarrow \frac{4x^3y}{36x^2y^3} = \frac{x^3y}{9x^2y^3}$

Use Exponent's rules: $\frac{x^a}{x^b} = x^{a-b} \rightarrow \frac{x^3}{x^2} = x^{3-2} = x$

Then: $\frac{4x^3y}{36x^2y^3} = \frac{xy}{9y^3} \rightarrow$ now cancel the common factor: $y \rightarrow \frac{xy}{9y^3} = \frac{x}{9y^2}$

2) Divide. $\frac{2x^{-5}}{9x^{-2}} =$

Use Exponent's rules: $\frac{x^a}{x^b} = \frac{1}{x^{b-a}} \rightarrow \frac{x^{-5}}{x^{-2}} = \frac{1}{x^{-2-(-5)}} = \frac{1}{x^{-2+5}} = \frac{1}{x^3}$

Then: $\frac{2x^{-5}}{9x^{-2}} = \frac{2}{9x^3}$

## ✍ *Simplify.*

1) $\frac{3^4 \times 3^7}{3^2 \times 3^8} =$

2) $\frac{5x}{10x^3} =$

3) $\frac{3x^3}{2x^5} =$

4) $\frac{12x^3}{14x^6} =$

5) $\frac{12x^3}{9y^8} =$

6) $\frac{25xy^4}{5x^6y^2} =$

7) $\frac{2x^4}{7x} =$

8) $\frac{16x^2y^8}{4x^3} =$

9) $\frac{12x^4}{15x^7y^9} =$

10) $\frac{12yx^4}{10yx^8} =$

11) $\frac{16x^4y}{9x^8y^2} =$

12) $\frac{5x^8}{20x^8} =$

# Powers of Products and Quotients

**Step-by-step guide:**

✓ For any nonzero numbers $a$ and $b$ and any integer $x$, $(ab)^x = a^x \times b^x$.

*Example:*

1) Simplify. $(3x^5y^4)^2 =$

Use Exponent's rules: $(x^a)^b = x^{a \times b}$

$(3x^5y^4)^2 = (3)^2(x^5)^2(y^4)^2 = 9x^{5 \times 2}y^{4 \times 2} = 9x^{10}y^8$

2) Simplify. $(\frac{2x}{3x^2})^2 =$

First cancel the common factor: $x \rightarrow (\frac{2x}{3x^2})^2 = (\frac{2}{3x})^2$

Use Exponent's rules: $(\frac{a}{b})^c = \frac{a^c}{b^c}$

Then: $(\frac{2}{3x})^2 = \frac{2^2}{(3x)^2} = \frac{4}{9x^2}$

✍ *Simplify.*

1) $(4x^3x^3)^2 =$

2) $(3x^3 \times 5x)^2 =$

3) $(10x^{11}y^3)^2 =$

4) $(9x^7y^5)^2 =$

5) $(4x^4y^6)^5 =$

6) $(3x \times 4y^3)^2 =$

7) $(\frac{5x}{x^2})^2 =$

8) $\left(\frac{x^4y^4}{x^2y^2}\right)^3 =$

9) $\left(\frac{25x}{5x^6}\right)^2 =$

10) $\left(\frac{x^8}{x^6y^2}\right)^2 =$

11) $\left(\frac{xy^2}{x^3y^3}\right)^{-2} =$

12) $\left(\frac{2xy^4}{x^3}\right)^2 =$

# Answers – Day 12

## Multiplication Property of Exponents

1) $3x^5$

2) $2x^3$

3) $25x^8$

4) $4x^3y$

5) $3x^8y^2$

6) $x^5y^7$

7) $8x^5y^4$

8) $36x^5y^4$

9) $21x^6y^8$

10) $63x^3y^8$

11) $28x^4y^7$

12) $24x^7y^6$

## Division Property of Exponents

1) $3$

2) $\dfrac{1}{2x^2}$

3) $\dfrac{3}{2x^2}$

4) $\dfrac{6}{7x^3}$

5) $\dfrac{4x^3}{3y^8}$

6) $\dfrac{5y^2}{x^5}$

7) $\dfrac{2x^3}{7}$

8) $\dfrac{4y^8}{x}$

9) $\dfrac{4}{5x^3y^9}$

10) $\dfrac{6}{5x^4}$

11) $\dfrac{16}{9x^4y}$

12) $\dfrac{1}{4}$

## Powers of Products and Quotients

1) $16x^{12}$

2) $225x^8$

3) $100x^{22}y^6$

4) $81x^{14}y^{10}$

5) $1,024x^{20}y^{30}$

6) $144x^2y^6$

7) $\dfrac{25}{x^2}$

8) $x^6y^6$

9) $\dfrac{25}{x^{10}}$

10) $\dfrac{x^4}{y^4}$

11) $x^4y^2$

12) $\dfrac{4y^8}{x^4}$

# Day 13: Exponents and Roots

## Math Topics that you'll learn today:

- ✓ Zero and Negative Exponents

- ✓ Negative Exponents and Negative Bases

- ✓ Scientific Notation

- ✓ Square Roots

*Mathematics is an independent world created out of pure intelligence.*

*~ William Woods Worth*

# Zero and Negative Exponents

**Step-by-step guide:**

 ✓  A negative exponent simply means that the base is on the wrong side of the fraction line, so you need to flip the base to the other side. For instance, "$x^{-2}$" (pronounced as "ecks to the minus two") just means "$x^2$" but underneath, as in $\frac{1}{x^2}$.

***Example:***

1) Evaluate. $\left(\frac{4}{9}\right)^{-2} =$

 Use Exponent's rules: $\frac{1}{x^b} = x^{-b} \rightarrow \left(\frac{4}{9}\right)^{-2} = \frac{1}{\left(\frac{4}{9}\right)^2} = \frac{1}{\frac{4^2}{9^2}}$

 Now use fraction rule: $\frac{1}{\frac{b}{c}} = \frac{c}{b} \rightarrow \frac{1}{\frac{4^2}{9^2}} = \frac{9^2}{4^2} = \frac{81}{16}$

2) Evaluate. $\left(\frac{5}{6}\right)^{-3} =$

 Use Exponent's rules: $\frac{1}{x^b} = x^{-b} \rightarrow \left(\frac{5}{6}\right)^{-3} = \frac{1}{\left(\frac{5}{6}\right)^3} = \frac{1}{\frac{5^3}{6^3}}$

 Now use fraction rule: $\frac{1}{\frac{b}{c}} = \frac{c}{b} \rightarrow \frac{1}{\frac{5^3}{6^3}} = \frac{6^3}{5^3} = \frac{216}{125}$

✎ ***Evaluate the following expressions.***

1) $2^{-3} =$

2) $3^{-3} =$

3) $7^{-3} =$

4) $6^{-3} =$

5) $8^{-3} =$

6) $9^{-2} =$

7) $10^{-3} =$

8) $10^{-9} =$

9) $\left(\frac{1}{2}\right)^{-1}$

10) $\left(\frac{1}{2}\right)^{-2} =$

11) $\left(\frac{1}{3}\right)^{-2} =$

12) $\left(\frac{2}{3}\right)^{-2} =$

# Negative Exponents and Negative Bases

## Step-by-step guide:

✓ Make the power positive.  A negative exponent is the reciprocal of that number with a positive exponent.
✓ The parenthesis is important!
✓ $5^{-2}$ is not the same as $(-5)^{-2}$

$$(-5)^{-2} = -\frac{1}{5^2} \text{ and } (-5)^{-2} = +\frac{1}{5^2}$$

## *Example:*

1) Simplify. $\left(\frac{3a}{2c}\right)^{-2} =$

Use Exponent's rules: $\frac{1}{x^b} = x^{-b} \rightarrow \left(\frac{3a}{2c}\right)^{-2} = \frac{1}{\left(\frac{3a}{2c}\right)^2} = \frac{1}{\frac{3^2a^2}{2^2c^2}}$

Now use fraction rule: $\frac{1}{\frac{b}{c}} = \frac{c}{b} \rightarrow \frac{1}{\frac{3^2a^2}{2^2c^2}} = \frac{2^2c^2}{3^2a^2}$

Then: $\frac{2^2c^2}{3^2a^2} = \frac{4c^2}{9a^2}$

2) Simplify. $\left(-\frac{5x}{3yz}\right)^{-3} =$

Use Exponent's rules: $\frac{1}{x^b} = x^{-b} \rightarrow \left(-\frac{5x}{3yz}\right)^{-3} = \frac{1}{\left(-\frac{5x}{3yz}\right)^3} = \frac{1}{-\frac{5^3x^3}{3^3y^3z^3}}$

Now use fraction rule: $\frac{1}{\frac{b}{c}} = \frac{c}{b} \rightarrow \frac{1}{-\frac{5^3x^3}{3^3y^3z^3}} = -\frac{3^3y^3z^3}{5^3x^3} = -\frac{27y^3z^3}{125x^3}$

## ✍ *Simplify.*

1) $-5x^{-2}y^{-3} =$

2) $20x^{-4}y^{-1} =$

3) $14a^{-6}b^{-7} =$

4) $-12x^2y^{-3} =$

5) $-\frac{25}{x^{-6}} =$

6) $\frac{7b}{-9c^{-4}} =$

7) $\frac{7ab}{a^{-3}b^{-1}} =$

8) $-\frac{5n^{-2}}{10p^{-3}} =$

9) $\frac{4ab^{-2}}{-3c^{-2}} =$

10) $\left(\frac{3a}{2c}\right)^{-2} =$

11) $\left(-\frac{5x}{3yz}\right)^{-3} =$

12) $\frac{4ab^{-2}}{-3c^{-2}} =$

13) $\left(-\frac{x^3}{x^4}\right)^{-2} =$

# Scientific Notation

**Step-by-step guide:**

✓ It is used to write very big or very small numbers in decimal form.
✓ In scientific notation all numbers are written in the form of:
$$m \times 10^n$$

| Decimal notation | Scientific notation |
|---|---|
| 5 | $5 \times 10^0$ |
| $-25{,}000$ | $-2.5 \times 10^4$ |
| 0.5 | $5 \times 10^{-1}$ |
| 2,122.456 | $2{,}122456 \times 10^3$ |

## *Example:*

1) Write **0.00012** in scientific notation.

First, move the decimal point to the right so that you have a number that is between 1 and 10. Then: $N = 1.2$

Second, determine how many places the decimal moved in step 1 by the power of 10. Then: $10^{-4} \rightarrow$ When the decimal moved to the right, the exponent is negative. Then: $0.00012 = 1.2 \times 10^{-4}$

2) Write **$8.3 \times 10^{-5}$** in standard notation.

$10^{-5} \rightarrow$ When the decimal moved to the right, the exponent is negative.
Then: $8.3 \times 10^{-5} = 0.000083$

## ✍ *Write each number in scientific notation.*

1) $0.000325 =$    3) $56{,}000{,}000 =$

2) $0.00023 =$    4) $21{,}000 =$

## ✍ *Write each number in standard notation.*

5) $3 \times 10^{-1} =$    7) $1.2 \times 10^3 =$

6) $5 \times 10^{-2} =$    8) $2 \times 10^{-4} =$

# Square Roots

**Step-by-step guide:**

   ✓ A square root of $x$ is a number $r$ whose square is: $r^2 = x$

        $r$ is a square root of $x$.

***Example:***

1) Find the square root of $\sqrt{225}$.

   First factor the number: $225 = 15^2$, Then: $\sqrt{225} = \sqrt{15^2}$

   Now use radical rule: $\sqrt[n]{a^n} = a$

   Then: $\sqrt{15^2} = 15$

2) Evaluate. $\sqrt{4} \times \sqrt{16} =$

   First factor the numbers: $4 = 2^2$ and $16 = 4^2$

   Then: $\sqrt{4} \times \sqrt{16} = \sqrt{2^2} \times \sqrt{4^2}$

   Now use radical rule: $\sqrt[n]{a^n} = a$, Then: $\sqrt{2^2} \times \sqrt{4^2} = 2 \times 4 = 8$

 ✎ ***Evaluate.***

1) $\sqrt{4} \times \sqrt{9} =$ _____

2) $\sqrt{25} \times \sqrt{64} =$ _____

3) $\sqrt{2} \times \sqrt{8} =$ _____

4) $\sqrt{6} \times \sqrt{6} =$ _____

5) $\sqrt{5} \times \sqrt{5} =$ _____

6) $\sqrt{8} \times \sqrt{8} =$ _____

7) $\sqrt{2} + \sqrt{2} =$ _____

8) $\sqrt{8} + \sqrt{8} =$ _____

9) $4\sqrt{5} - 2\sqrt{5} =$ _____

10) $3\sqrt{3} \times 2\sqrt{3} =$ _____

11) $8\sqrt{2} \times 2\sqrt{2} =$ _____

12) $6\sqrt{3} - \sqrt{12} =$ _____

# Answers – Day 13

## Zero and Negative Exponents

1) $\frac{1}{8}$

2) $\frac{1}{27}$

3) $\frac{1}{343}$

4) $\frac{1}{216}$

5) $\frac{1}{512}$

6) $\frac{1}{81}$

7) $\frac{1}{1,000}$

8) $\frac{1}{1,000,000,000}$

9) $2$

10) $4$

11) $9$

12) $\frac{9}{4}$

## Negative Exponents and Negative Bases

1) $-\frac{5}{x^2 y^3}$

2) $\frac{20}{x^4 y}$

3) $\frac{14}{a^6 b^7}$

4) $-\frac{12x^2}{y^3}$

5) $-25x^6$

6) $-\frac{7bc^4}{9}$

7) $7a^4 b^2$

8) $-\frac{p^3}{2n^2}$

9) $-\frac{4ac^2}{3b^2}$

10) $\frac{4c^2}{9a^2}$

11) $-\frac{27y^3 z^3}{125x^3}$

12) $-\frac{4ac^2}{3b^2}$

13) $x^2$

## Scientific Notation

1) $3.25 \times 10^{-4}$

2) $2.3 \times 10^{-4}$

3) $5.6 \times 10^7$

4) $2.1 \times 10^4$

5) $0.3$

6) $0.05$

7) $1,200$

8) $0.0002$

## Square Roots

1) $6$

2) $40$

3) $4$

4) $6$

5) $5$

6) $8$

7) $2\sqrt{2}$

8) $2\sqrt{8}$

9) $2\sqrt{5}$

10) $18$

11) $32$

12) $4\sqrt{3}$

# Day 14: Expressions and Variables

**Math Topics that you'll learn today:**

- ✓ Simplifying Variable Expressions

- ✓ Simplifying Polynomial Expressions

- ✓ Translate Phrases into an Algebraic Statement

*Mathematics is, as it were, a sensuous logic, and relates to philosophy as do the arts, music, and plastic art to poetry. – K.*

*Shegel*

# Simplifying Variable Expressions

**Step-by-step guide:**

- ✓ In algebra, a variable is a letter used to stand for a number. The most common letters are: $x, y, z, a, b, c, m,$ and $n$.
- ✓ algebraic expression is an expression contains integers, variables, and the math operations such as addition, subtraction, multiplication, division, etc.
- ✓ In an expression, we can combine "like" terms. (values with same variable and same power)

**Examples:**

1) Simplify this expression. $(10x + 2x + 3) =?$
   Combine like terms. Then: $(10x + 2x + 3) = 12x + 3$ (remember you cannot combine variables and numbers.

2) Simplify this expression. $12 - 3x^2 + 9x + 5x^2 =?$
   Combine "like" terms: $-3x^2 + 5x^2 = 2x^2$

   Then: $12 - 3x^2 + 9x + 5x^2 = 12 + 2x^2 + 9x$. Write in standard form (biggest powers first): $2x^2 + 9x + 12$

✍ *Simplify each expression.*

1) $(2x + x + 3 + 24) =$

2) $(-28x - 20x + 24) =$

3) $7x + 3 - 3x =$

4) $-2 - x^2 - 6x^2 =$

5) $3 + 10x^2 + 2 =$

6) $8x^2 + 6x + 7x^2 =$

7) $5x^2 - 12x^2 + 8x =$

8) $2x^2 - 2x - x =$

9) $4x + (12 - 30x) =$

10) $10x + (80x - 48) =$

11) $(-18x - 54) - 5 =$

12) $2x^2 + (-8x) =$

# Simplifying Polynomial Expressions

**Step-by-step guide:**

✓ In mathematics, a polynomial is an expression consisting of variables and coefficients that involves only the operations of addition, subtraction, multiplication, and non-negative integer exponents of variables.

$$P(x) = a_n x^n + a_{n-1} x^{n-1} + \ldots + a_2 x^2 + a_1 x + a_0$$

**Examples:**

1) Simplify this Polynomial Expressions. $4x^2 - 5x^3 + 15x^4 - 12x^3 =$

Combine "like" terms: $-5x^3 - 12x^3 = -17x^3$

Then: $4x^2 - 5x^3 + 15x^4 - 12x^3 = 4x^2 - 17x^3 + 15x^4$

Then write in standard form: $4x^2 - 17x^3 + 15x^4 = 15x^4 - 17x^3 + 4x^2$

2) Simplify this expression. $(2x^2 - x^4) - (4x^4 - x^2) =$

First use distributive property: → multiply $(-)$ into $(4x^4 - x^2)$

$(2x^2 - x^4) - (4x^4 - x^2) = 2x^2 - x^4 - 4x^4 + x^2$

Then combine "like" terms: $2x^2 - x^4 - 4x^4 + x^2 = 3x^2 - 5x^4$

And write in standard form: $3x^2 - 5x^4 = -5x^4 + 3x^2$

✎ *Simplify each polynomial.*

1) $(2x^3 + 5x^2) - (12x + 2x^2) =$ _____

2) $(2x^5 + 2x^3) - (7x^3 + 6x^2) =$ _____

3) $(12x^4 + 4x^2) - (2x^2 - 6x^4) =$ _____

4) $14x - 3x^2 - 2(6x^2 + 6x^3) =$ _____

5) $(5x^3 - 3) + 5(2x^2 - 3x^3) =$ _____

6) $(4x^3 - 2x) - 2(4x^3 - 2x^4) =$ _____

7) $2(4x - 3x^3) - 3(3x^3 + 4x^2) =$ _____

8) $(2x^2 - 2x) - (2x^3 + 5x^2) =$ _____

# Translate Phrases into an Algebraic Statement

**Step-by-step guide:**

Translating key words and phrases into algebraic expressions:

- ✓ Addition: plus, more than, the sum of, etc.
- ✓ Subtraction: minus, less than, decreased, etc.
- ✓ Multiplication: times, product, multiplied, etc.
- ✓ Division: quotient, divided, ratio, etc.

**Examples:**

Write an algebraic expression for each phrase.

1) Eight more than a number is **20**.
   More than mean plus a number $= x$
   Then: $8 + x = 20$

2) 5 times the sum of **8** and $x$.
   Sum of 8 and $x$: $8 + x$. Times means multiplication. Then: $5 \times (8 + x)$

✎ **_Write an algebraic expression for each phrase._**

1) 4 multiplied by $x$. _____

2) Subtract 8 from $y$. _____

3) 6 divided by $x$. _____

4) 12 decreased by $y$. _____

5) Add $y$ to 9. _____

6) The square of 5. _____

7) $x$ raised to the fourth power. _____

8) The sum of nine and a number. _____

9) The difference between sixty–four and $y$. _____

10) The quotient of twelve and a number. _____

11) The quotient of the square of $x$ and 7. _____

12) The difference between $x$ and 8 is 22. _____

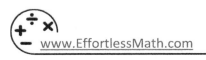

# Answers – Day 14

### *Simplifying Variable Expressions*

1) $3x + 27$

2) $-48x + 24$

3) $4x + 3$

4) $-7x^2 - 2$

5) $10x^2 + 5$

6) $15x^2 + 6x$

7) $-7x^2 + 8x$

8) $2x^2 - 3x$

9) $-26x + 12$

10) $90x - 48$

11) $-18x - 59$

12) $2x^2 - 8x$

### *Simplifying Polynomial Expressions*

1) $2x^3 + 3x^2 - 12x$

2) $2x^5 - 5x^3 - 6x^2$

3) $18x^4 + 2x^2$

4) $-12x^3 - 15x^2 + 14x$

5) $-10x^3 + 10x^2 - 3$

6) $4x^4 - 4x^3 - 2x$

7) $-15x^3 - 12x^2 + 8x$

8) $-2x^3 - 3x^2 - 2x$

### *Translate Phrases into an Algebraic Statement*

1) $4x$

2) $y - 8$

3) $\frac{6}{x}$

4) $12 - y$

5) $y + 9$

6) $5^2$

7) $x^4$

8) $9 + x$

9) $64 - y$

10) $\frac{12}{x}$

11) $\frac{x^2}{7}$

12) $x - 8 = 22$

# Day 15: Evaluating Variables

**Math Topics that you'll learn today:**

- ✓ The Distributive Property

- ✓ Evaluating One Variable

- ✓ Evaluating Two Variables

- ✓ Combining like Terms

*Mathematics is on the artistic side a creation of new rhythms, orders, designs, harmonies, and on the knowledge side, is a systematic study of various rhythms, orders. ~ William L. Schaaf*

# The Distributive Property

**Step-by-step guide:**

✓ Distributive Property:
$$a(b + c) = ab + ac$$

**Examples:**

1) Simply. $(5x - 3)(-5) =$

Use Distributive Property formula: $a(b + c) = ab + ac$
$(5x - 3)(-5) = -25x + 15$

2) Simply. $(-8)(2x - 8) =$

Use Distributive Property formula: $a(b + c) = ab + ac$
$(-8)(2x - 8) = -16x + 64$

✏ *Use the distributive property to simply each expression.*

1) $2(2 + 3x) =$

2) $3(5 + 5x) =$

3) $4(3x - 8) =$

4) $(6x - 2)(-2) =$

5) $(-3)(x + 2) =$

6) $(2 + 2x)5 =$

7) $(-4)(4 - 2x) =$

8) $-(-2 - 5x) =$

9) $(-6x + 2)(-1) =$

10) $(-5)(x - 2) =$

11) $-(7 - 3x) =$

12) $8(8 + 2x) =$

# Evaluating One Variable

**Step-by-step guide:**

- ✓ To evaluate one variable expression, find the variable and substitute a number for that variable.
- ✓ Perform the arithmetic operations.

**Examples:**

1) Solve this expression. $12 - 2x$, $x = -1$

First substitute $-1$ for $x$, then:

$12 - 2x = 12 - 2(-1) = 12 + 2 = 14$

2) Solve this expression. $-8 + 5x$, $x = 3$

First substitute 3 for $x$, then:

$-8 + 5x = -8 + 5(3) = -8 + 15 = 7$

✎ *Evaluate each expression using the value given.*

1) $5 + x$, $x = 2$

2) $x - 2$, $x = 4$

3) $8x + 1$, $x = 9$

4) $x - 12$, $x = -1$

5) $9 - x$, $x = 3$

6) $x + 2$, $x = 5$

7) $3x + 7$, $x = 6$

8) $x + (-5)$, $x = -2$

9) $3x + 6$, $x = 4$

10) $4x + 6$, $x = -1$

11) $10 + 2x - 6$, $x = 3$

12) $10 - 3x$, $x = 8$

# Evaluating Two Variables

**Step-by-step guide:**

✓ To evaluate an algebraic expression, substitute a number for each variable and perform the arithmetic operations.

**Examples:**

1) Solve this expression.  $-3x + 5y$ , $x = 2, y = -1$

First substitute 2 for $x$, and $-1$ for $y$ , then:

$-3x + 5y = -3(2) + 5(-1) = -6 - 5 = -11$

2) Solve this expression.  $2(a - 2b), a = -1, b = 3$

First substitute $-1$ for $a$, and 3 for $b$ , then:

$2(a - 2b) = 2a - 4b = 2(-1) - 4(3) = -2 - 12 = -14$

✎ *Evaluate each expression using the values given.*

1)  $2x + 4y$,
   $x = 3, y = 2$

2)  $8x + 5y$,
   $x = 1, y = 5$

3)  $-2a + 4b$,
   $a = 6, b = 3$

4)  $4x + 7 - 2y$,
   $x = 7, y = 6$

5)  $5z + 12 - 4k$,
   $z = 5 , k = 2$

6)  $2(-x - 2y)$,
   $x = 6, y = 9$

7)  $18a + 2b$,
   $a = 2, b = 8$

8)  $4x \div 3y$,
   $x = 3, y = 2$

9)  $2x + 15 + 4y$,
   $x = -2, y = 4$

10) $4a - (15 - b)$,
   $a = 4, b = 6$

11) $5z + 19 + 8k$,
   $z = -5, k = 4$

12) $xy + 12 + 5x$,
   $x = 7, y = 2$

# Combining like Terms

## Step-by-step guide:

- ✓ Terms are separated by "+" and "-" signs.
- ✓ Like terms are terms with same variables and same powers.
- ✓ Be sure to use the "+" or "-" that is in front of the coefficient.

## Examples:

1) Simplify this expression. $(-5)(8x - 6) =$

   Use Distributive Property formula: $a(b + c) = a + ac$
   $(-5)(8x - 6) = -40x + 30$

2) Simplify this expression. $(-3)(2x - 2) + 6 =$

   First use Distributive Property formula: $a(b + c) = ab + ac$
   $(-3)(2x - 2) + 6 = -6x + 6 + 6$

   And Combining like Terms:

   $-6x + 6 + 6 = -6x + 12$

✎ *Simplify each expression.*

1) $2x + x + 2 =$

2) $2(5x - 3) =$

3) $7x - 2x + 8 =$

4) $(-4)(3x - 5) =$

5) $9x - 7x - 5 =$

6) $16x - 5 + 8x =$

7) $5 - (5x + 6) =$

8) $-12x + 7 - 10x =$

9) $7x - 11 - 2x + 2 =$

10) $12x + 4x - 21 =$

11) $5 + 2x - 8 =$

12) $(-2x + 6)^2 =$

# Answers – Day 15

## The Distributive Property

1) $6x + 4$

2) $15x + 15$

3) $12x - 32$

4) $-12x + 4$

5) $-3x - 6$

6) $10x + 10$

7) $8x - 16$

8) $5x + 2$

9) $6x - 2$

10) $-5x + 10$

11) $3x - 7$

12) $16x + 64$

## Evaluating One Variable

1) 7

2) 2

3) 73

4) $-13$

5) 6

6) 7

7) 25

8) $-7$

9) 18

10) 2

11) 10

12) $-14$

## Evaluating Two Variables

1) 14

2) 33

3) 0

4) 23

5) 29

6) $-48$

7) 52

8) 2

9) 27

10) 7

11) 26

12) 61

## Combining like Terms

1) $3x + 2$

2) $10x - 6$

3) $5x + 8$

4) $-12x + 20$

5) $2x - 5$

6) $24x - 5$

7) $-5x - 1$

8) $-22x + 7$

9) $5x - 9$

10) $16x - 21$

11) $2x - 3$

12) $4x^2 - 24x + 36$

# Day 16: Equations and Inequalities

## Math Topics that you'll learn today:

- ✓ One–Step Equations

- ✓ Multi–Step Equations

- ✓ Graphing Single–Variable Inequalities

*"Life is a math equation. In order to gain the most, you have to know how to convert negatives into positives."*

*– Anonymous*

# One–Step Equations

**Step-by-step guide:**

✓ The values of two expressions on both sides of an equation are equal. $ax + b = c$

✓ You only need to perform one Math operation in order to solve the one-step equations.

✓ To solve one-step equation, find the inverse (opposite) operation is being performed.

✓ The inverse operations are:
- Addition and subtraction
- Multiplication and division

**Examples:**

1) Solve this equation. $x + 24 = 0$, $x = ?$
   Here, the operation is addition and its inverse operation is subtraction. To solve this equation, subtract 24 from both sides of the equation: $x + 24 - 24 = 0 - 24$
   Then simplify: $x + 24 - 24 = 0 - 24 \rightarrow x = -24$

2) Solve this equation. $3x = 15$, $x = ?$
   Here, the operation is multiplication (variable $x$ is multiplied by 3) and its inverse operation is division. To solve this equation, divide both sides of equation by 3:
   $$3x = 15 \rightarrow 3x \div 3 = 15 \div 3 \rightarrow x = 5$$

✍ *Solve each equation.*

1) $16 = -4 + x$, $x =$ _____

2) $x - 4 = -25$, $x =$ _____

3) $x + 12 = -9$, $x =$ _____

4) $14 = 18 - x$, $x =$ _____

5) $2 + x = -14$, $x =$ _____

6) $x - 5 = 15$, $x =$ _____

7) $25 = x - 5$, $x =$ _____

8) $x - 3 = -12$, $x =$ _____

9) $x - 12 = 12$, $x =$ _____

10) $x - 12 = -25$, $x =$ _____

11) $x - 13 = 32$, $x =$ _____

12) $-55 = x - 18$, $x =$ _____

# Multi–Step Equations

**Step-by-step guide:**

- ✓ Combine "like" terms on one side.
- ✓ Bring variables to one side by adding or subtracting.
- ✓ Simplify using the inverse of addition or subtraction.
- ✓ Simplify further by using the inverse of multiplication or division.

**Examples:**

1) Solve this equation. $-(2-x) = 5$

First use Distributive Property: $-(2-x) = -2+x$

Now solve by adding 2 to both sides of the equation. $-2+x = 5 \rightarrow -2+x+2 = 5+2$

Now simplify: $-2+x+2 = 5+2 \rightarrow x = 7$

2) Solve this equation. $4x + 10 = 25 - x$

First bring variables to one side by adding $x$ to both sides.

$4x + 10 + x = 25 - x + x \rightarrow 5x + 10 = 25$ . Now, subtract 10 from both sides:

$5x + 10 - 10 = 25 - 10 \rightarrow 5x = 15$

Now, divide both sides by 5: $5x = 15 \rightarrow 5x \div 5 = \frac{15}{5} \rightarrow x = 3$

✐ *Solve each equation.*

1) $-3(2 + x) = 3$

2) $-2(4 + x) = 4$

3) $20 = -(x - 8)$

4) $2(2 - 2x) = 20$

5) $-12 = -(2x + 8)$

6) $5(2 + x) = 5$

7) $2(x - 14) = 4$

8) $-28 = 2x + 12x$

9) $3x + 15 = -x - 5$

10) $2(3 + 2x) = -18$

11) $12 - 2x = -8 - x$

12) $10 - 3x = 14 + x$

# Graphing Single–Variable Inequalities

**Step-by-step guide:**

- ✓ Inequality is similar to equations and uses symbols for "less than" (<) and "greater than" (>).
- ✓ To solve inequalities, we need to isolate the variable. (like in equations)
- ✓ To graph an inequality, find the value of the inequality on the number line.
- ✓ For less than or greater than draw open circle on the value of the variable.
- ✓ If there is an equal sign too, then use filled circle.
- ✓ Draw a line to the right or to the left for greater or less than.

**Examples:**

1) Draw a graph for $x > 2$

Since, the variable is greater than 2, then we need to find 2 and draw an open circle above it. Then, draw a line to the right.

Graph this inequality. $x < 5$

## ✍ Draw a graph for each inequality.

1) $x > -1$

2) $x < 3$

3) $x < -5$

4) $x > -2$

5) $x < 0$

# Answers – Day 16

### One–Step Equations

1) 20
2) −21
3) −21
4) 4
5) −16
6) 20

7) 30
8) −9
9) 24
10) −13
11) 45
12) −37

### Multi–Step Equations

1) −3
2) −6
3) −12
4) −4
5) 2
6) −1

7) 16
8) −2
9) −5
10) −6
11) 20
12) −1

### Graphing Single–Variable Inequalities

# Day 17: Solving Inequalities

## Math Topics that you'll learn today:

- ✓ One–Step Inequalities

- ✓ Multi–Step Inequalities

*Go down deep enough into anything and you will find mathematics." – Dean Schlicter*

# One–Step Inequalities

**Step-by-step guide:**

✓ Similar to equations, first isolate the variable by using inverse operation.
✓ For dividing or multiplying both sides by negative numbers, flip the direction of the inequality sign.

## Examples:

1) Solve and graph the inequality. $x + 2 \geq 3$.

Subtract 2 from both sides. $x + 2 \geq 3 \rightarrow x + 2 - 2 \geq 3 - 2$, then: $x \geq 1$

2) Solve this inequality. $x - 1 \leq 2$

Add 1 to both sides. $x - 1 \leq 2 \rightarrow x - 1 + 1 \leq 2 + 1$, then: $x \leq 3$

✎ *Solve each inequality and graph it.*

1) $2x \geq 12$

2) $4 + x \leq 5$

3) $x + 3 \leq -3$

4) $4x \geq 16$

5) $9x \leq 18$

# Multi–Step Inequalities

**Step-by-step guide:**

✓ Isolate the variable.
✓ Simplify using the inverse of addition or subtraction.
✓ Simplify further by using the inverse of multiplication or division.

**Examples:**

1) Solve this inequality. $2x - 2 \leq 6$

First add 2 to both sides: $2x - 2 + 2 \leq 6 + 2 \rightarrow 2x \leq 8$

Now, divide both sides by 2: $2x \leq 8 \rightarrow x \leq 4$

2) Solve this inequality. $2x - 4 \leq 8$

First add 4 to both sides: $2x - 4 + 4 \leq 8 + 4$

Then simplify: $2x - 4 + 4 \leq 8 + 4 \rightarrow 2x \leq 12$

Now divide both sides by 2: $\frac{2x}{2} \leq \frac{12}{2} \rightarrow x \leq 6$

✍ *Solve each inequality.*

1) $2x - 8 \leq 6$

2) $8x - 2 \leq 14$

3) $-5 + 3x \leq 10$

4) $2(x - 3) \leq 6$

5) $7x - 5 \leq 9$

6) $4x - 21 < 19$

7) $2x - 3 < 21$

8) $17 - 3x \geq -13$

9) $9 + 4x < 21$

10) $3 + 2x \geq 19$

11) $6 + 2x < 32$

12) $4x - 1 < 7$

# Answers – Day 17

### *One–Step Inequalities*

1)

2)

3)

4)

5)

### *Multi–Step inequalities*

1) $x \leq 7$
2) $x \leq 2$
3) $x \leq 5$
4) $x \leq 6$
5) $x \leq 2$
6) $x < 10$
7) $x < 12$
8) $x \leq 10$
9) $x < 3$
10) $x \geq 8$
11) $x < 13$
12) $x < 2$

# Day 18: Lines and Slope

**Math Topics that you'll learn today:**

- ✓ Finding Slope

- ✓ Graphing Lines Using Slope–Intercept Form

- ✓ Graphing Lines Using Standard Form

*"Nature is written in mathematical language." - Galileo Galilei*

# Finding Slope

**Step-by-step guide:**

- ✓ The slope of a line represents the direction of a line on the coordinate plane.
- ✓ A coordinate plane contains two perpendicular number lines. The horizontal line is $x$ and the vertical line is $y$. The point at which the two axes intersect is called the origin. An ordered pair $(x, y)$ shows the location of a point.
- ✓ A line on coordinate plane can be drawn by connecting two points.
- ✓ To find the slope of a line, we need two points.
- ✓ The slope of a line with two points A $(x_1, y_1)$ and B $(x_2, y_2)$ can be found by using this formula: $\frac{y_2 - y_1}{x_2 - x_1} = \frac{rise}{run}$

**Examples:**

1) Find the slope of the line through these two points: $(2, -10)$ and $(3, 6)$.

Slope $= \frac{y_2 - y_1}{x_2 - x_1}$. Let $(x_1, y_1)$ be $(2, -10)$ and $(x_2, y_2)$ be $(3, 6)$. Then: slope $= \frac{y_2 - y_1}{x_2 - x_1} = \frac{6-(-10)}{3-2} = \frac{6+10}{1} = \frac{16}{1} = 16$

2) Find the slope of the line containing two points $(8, 3)$ and $(-4, 9)$.

Slope $= \frac{y_2 - y_1}{x_2 - x_1} \rightarrow (x_1, y_1) = (8, 3)$ and $(x_2, y_2) = (-4, 9)$. Then: slope$= \frac{y_2 - y_1}{x_2 - x_1} = \frac{9-3}{-4-8} = \frac{6}{-12} = \frac{1}{-2} = -\frac{1}{2}$

✎ *Find the slope of the line through each pair of points.*

1) $(1, 1), (2, 3)$

2) $(-1, 2), (0, 3)$

3) $(3, -1), (2, 3)$

4) $(-2, -1), (0, 5)$

5) $(5, 1), (2, 4)$

6) $(-3, 1), (-2, 4)$

7) $(6, 2), (7, 4)$

8) $(6, -5), (3, 4)$

9) $(12, -9), (11, -8)$

10) $(7, 4), (5, -2)$

11) $(1, 1), (3, 5)$

12) $(7, -12), (5, 10)$

# Graphing Lines Using Slope–Intercept Form

**Step-by-step guide:**

✓ Slope-intercept form of a line: given the slope $m$ and the $y$-intercept (the intersection of the line and y-axis) $b$, then the equation of the line is:

$$y = mx + b$$

**Example:** *Sketch the graph of* $y = 8x - 3$.

To graph this line, we need to find two points. When $x$ is zero the value of $y$ is $-3$. And when y is zero the value of $x$ is $\frac{3}{8}$. $x = 0 \rightarrow y = 8(0) - 3 = -3$, $y = 0 \rightarrow 0 = 8x - 3 \rightarrow x = \frac{3}{8}$

Now, we have two points: $(0, -3)$ and $(\frac{3}{8}, 0)$. Find the points and graph the line. Remember that the slope of the line is 8.

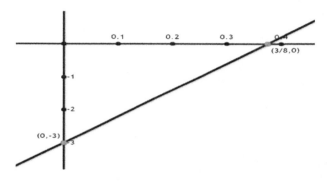

✍ *Sketch the graph of each line.*

1) $y = \frac{1}{2}x - 4$

2) $y = 2x$

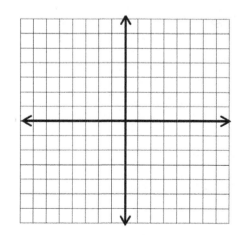

# Graphing Lines Using Standard Form

**Step-by-step guide:**

- ✓ Find the $x$ –intercept of the line by putting zero for $y$.
- ✓ Find the $y$ –intercept of the line by putting zero for the $x$.
- ✓ Connect these two points.

**Example:**

Sketch the graph of $x - y = -5$.

First isolate $y$ for $x$: $x - y = -5 \rightarrow y = x + 5$

Find the $x$–intercept of the line by putting zero for $y$.

$y = x + 5 \rightarrow x + 5 = 0 \rightarrow x = -5$

Find the $y$–intercept of the line by putting zero for the $x$.

$y = 0 + 5 \rightarrow y = 5$

Then: $x$–intercept: $(-5, 0)$ and $y$–intercept: $(0, 5)$

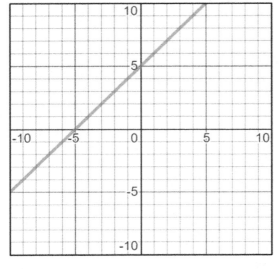

**Sketch the graph of each line.**

1) $y = 3x - 2$         2) $y = -x + 1$         3) $x + y = 4$

            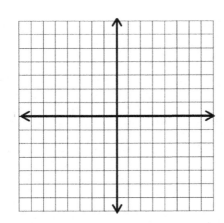

# Answers – Day 18

### Finding Slope

1) 2

2) 1

3) −4

4) 3

5) −1

6) 3

7) 2

8) −3

9) −1

10) 3

11) 2

12) −11

### Graphing Lines Using Slope–Intercept Form

1)

2)

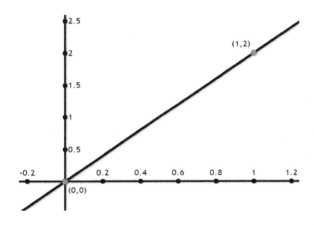

## Graphing Lines Using Standard Form

1) $y = 3x - 2$

2) $y = -x + 1$

3) $x + y = 4$

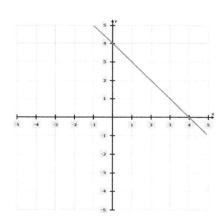

# Day 19: Linear Equations and Inequalities

## Math Topics that you'll learn today:

- ✓ Writing Linear Equations

- ✓ Graphing Linear Inequalities

- ✓ Finding Midpoint

- ✓ Finding Distance of Two Points

*Mathematics is a game played according to certain rules with meaningless marks on paper. ~ David Hilbert*

# Writing Linear Equations

**Step-by-step guide:**

- ✓ The equation of a line: $y = mx + b$
- ✓ Identify the slope.
- ✓ Find the y-intercept. This can be done by substituting the slope and the coordinates of a point $(x, y)$ on the line.

***Example:***

1) What is the equation of the line that passes through $(2, -2)$ and has a slope of 7?

   The general slope-intercept form of the equation of a line is $y = mx + b$, where $m$ is the slope and $b$ is the y-intercept.

   By substitution of the given point and given slope, we have: $-2 = (2)(7) + b$

   So, $b = -2 - 14 = -16$, and the required equation is $y = 2x - 16$.

2) Write the equation of the line through $(2, 1)$ and $(-1, 4)$.

   Slope $= \frac{y_2 - y_1}{x_2 - x_1} = \frac{4 - 1}{-1 - 2} = \frac{3}{-3} = -1 \to m = -1$

   To find the value of $b$, you can use either points. The answer will be the same: $y = -x + b$

   $(2, 1) \to 1 = -2 + b \to b = 3$

   $(-1, 4) \to 4 = -(-1) + b \to b = 3$

   The equation of the line is: $y = -x + 3$

✎ ***Write the equation of the line through the given points.***

1) through: $(1, -2), (2, 3)$

2) through: $(-2, 1), (1, 4)$

3) through: $(-2, 1), (0, 5)$

4) through: $(5, 4), (2, 1)$

5) through: $(-4, 9), (3, 2)$

6) through: $(8, 3), (7, 2)$

7) through: $(7, -2), (5, 2)$

8) through: $(-3, 9), (5, -7)$

# Graphing Linear Inequalities

## Step-by-step guide:

- ✓ First, graph the "equals" line.
- ✓ Choose a testing point. (it can be any point on both sides of the line.)
- ✓ Put the value of $(x, y)$ of that point in the inequality. If that works, that part of the line is the solution. If the values don't work, then the other part of the line is the solution.

### *Example:*

Sketch the graph of $y < 2x - 3$. First, graph the line:

$y = 2x - 3$. The slope is 2 and y-intercept is $-3$. Then, choose a testing point. The easiest point to test is the origin: $(0, 0)$

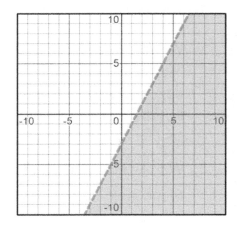

$$(0, 0) \rightarrow y < 2x - 3 \rightarrow 0 < 2(0) - 3 \rightarrow 0 < -3$$

0 is not less than $-3$. So, the other part of the line (on the right side) is the solution.

### ✍ *Sketch the graph of each linear inequality.*

1) $y > 3x - 1$           2) $y < -x + 4$           3) $y \leq -5x + 8$

  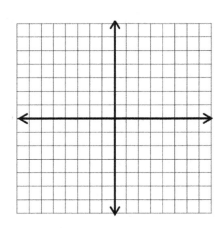

# Finding Midpoint

**Step-by-step guide:**

- ✓ The middle of a line segment is its midpoint.
- ✓ The Midpoint of two endpoints A $(x_1, y_1)$ and B $(x_2, y_2)$ can be found using this formula: M $(\frac{x_1+x_2}{2}, \frac{y_1+y_2}{2})$

*Example:*

1) Find the midpoint of the line segment with the given endpoints. $(4, -5), (0, 9)$

Midpoint $= (\frac{x_1+x_2}{2}, \frac{y_1+y_2}{2}) \rightarrow (x_1, y_1) = (4, -5)$ and $(x_2, y_2) = (0, 9)$

Midpoint $= (\frac{4+0}{2}, \frac{-5+9}{2}) \rightarrow (\frac{4}{2}, \frac{4}{2}) \rightarrow M(2, 2)$

2) Find the midpoint of the line segment with the given endpoints. $(6, 7), (4, -5)$

Midpoint $= (\frac{x_1+x_2}{2}, \frac{y_1+y_2}{2}) \rightarrow (x_1, y_1) = (6, 7)$ and $(x_2, y_2) = (4, -5)$

Midpoint $= (\frac{6+4}{2}, \frac{7-5}{2}) \rightarrow (\frac{10}{2}, \frac{2}{2}) \rightarrow (5, 1)$

✎ *Find the midpoint of the line segment with the given endpoints.*

1) $(-2, -2), (0, 2)$　　　　　　　　　7) $(5, 0), (-5, 8)$

2) $(5, 1), (-2, 4)$　　　　　　　　　　8) $(-6, 4), (-2, 0)$

3) $(4, -1), (0, 3)$　　　　　　　　　　9) $(-3, 4), (9, -6)$

4) $(-3, 5), (-1, 3)$　　　　　　　　　10) $(2, 8), (6, -2)$

5) $(3, -2), (7, -6)$　　　　　　　　　11) $(4, 7), (-6, 5)$

6) $(-4, -3), (2, -7)$　　　　　　　　12) $(9, 3), (-1, -7)$

## Finding Distance of Two Points

**Step-by-step guide:**

✓ Distance of two points A $(x_1, y_1)$ and B $(x_2, y_2)$: $d = \sqrt{(x_1 - x_2)^2 + (y_1 - y_2)^2}$

**Example:**

1) Find the distance between of $(0, 8), (-4, 5)$.

Use distance of two points formula: $d = \sqrt{(x_1 - x_2)^2 + (y_1 - y_2)^2}$

$(x_1, y_1) = (0, 8)$ and $(x_2, y_2) = (-4, 5)$. Then: $d = \sqrt{(x_1 - x_2)^2 + (y_1 - y_2)^2} \rightarrow$

$d = \sqrt{(0 - (-4))^2 + (8 - 5)^2} = \sqrt{(4)^2 + (3)^2} = \sqrt{16 + 9} = \sqrt{25} = 5 \rightarrow d = 5$

2) Find the distance of two points $(4, 2)$ and $(-5, -10)$.

Use distance of two points formula: $d = \sqrt{(x_1 - x_2)^2 + (y_1 - y_2)^2}$

$(x_1, y_1) = (4, 2)$, and $(x_2, y_2) = (-5, -10)$

Then: $d = \sqrt{(x_1 - x_2)^2 + (y_1 - y_2)^2} \rightarrow d = \sqrt{(4 - (-5))^2 + (2 - (-10))^2} =$

$\sqrt{(9)^2 + (12)^2} = \sqrt{81 + 144} = \sqrt{225} = 15$. Then: $d = 15$

### ✎ Find the distance between each pair of points.

1) $(2, 1), (-1, -3)$

2) $(-2, -1), (2, 2)$

3) $(-1, 0), (5, 8)$

4) $(-4, -1), (1, 11)$

5) $(3, -2), (-6, -14)$

6) $(-6, 0), (-2, 3)$

7) $(3, 2), (11, 17)$

8) $(-6, -10), (6, -1)$

9) $(5, 9), (-11, -3)$

10) $(9, -3), (3, -11)$

11) $(2, 0), (12, 24)$

12) $(8, 4), (3, -8)$

# Answers – Day 19

### *Writing Linear Equations*

1) $y = 5x - 7$
2) $y = x + 3$
3) $y = 2x + 5$
4) $y = x - 1$

5) $y = -x + 5$
6) $y = x - 5$
7) $y = -2x + 12$
8) $y = -2x + 3$

### *Graphing Linear Inequalities*

1) $y > 3x - 1$

2) $y < -x + 4$

3) $y \leq -5x + 8$

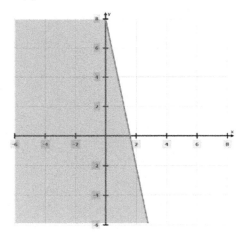

## Finding Midpoint

1) $(-1, 0)$
2) $(1.5, 2.5)$
3) $(2, 1)$
4) $(-2, 4)$

5) $(5, -4)$
6) $(-1, -5)$
7) $(0, 4)$
8) $(-4, 2)$

9) $(3, -1)$
10) $(4, 3)$
11) $(-1, 6)$
12) $(4, -2)$

## Finding Distance of Two Points

1) 5
2) 5
3) 10
4) 13

5) 15
6) 5
7) 17
8) 15

9) 20
10) 10
11) 26
12) 13

# Day 20: Polynomials

**Math Topics that you'll learn today:**

- ✓ Writing Polynomials in Standard Form

- ✓ Simplifying Polynomials

- ✓ Adding and Subtracting Polynomials

*Mathematics is the supreme judge; from its decisions there is no appeal. –Tobias Dantzig*

# Writing Polynomials in Standard Form

**Step-by-step guide:**

&#10003; A polynomial function $f(x)$ of degree $n$ is of the form
$$f(x) = a_n x^n + a_{n-1} x_{n-1} + \cdots + a_1 x + a_0$$
&#10003; The first term is the one with the biggest power!

***Example:***

1) Write this polynomial in standard form. $-12 + 3x^2 - 6x^4 =$

The first term is the one with the biggest power: $-12 + 3x^2 - 6x^4 = -6x^4 + 3x^2 - 12$

2) Write this polynomial in standard form. $5x^2 - 9x^5 + 8x^3 - 11 =$

The first term is the one with the biggest power: $5x^2 - 9x^5 + 8x^3 - 11 =$
$-9x^5 + 8x^3 + 5x^2 - 11$

&#9998; ***Write each polynomial in standard form.***

1) $9x - 7x =$

2) $-3 + 16x - 16x =$

3) $3x^2 - 5x^3 =$

4) $3 + 4x^3 - 3 =$

5) $2x^2 + 1x - 6x^3 =$

6) $-x^2 + 2x^3 =$

7) $2x + 4x^3 - 2x^2 =$

8) $-2x^2 + 4x - 6x^3 =$

9) $2x^2 + 2 - 5x =$

10) $12 - 7x + 9x^4 =$

11) $5x^2 + 13x - 2x^3 =$

12) $10 + 6x^2 - x^3 =$

# Simplifying Polynomials

**Step-by-step guide:**

✓ Find "like" terms. (they have same variables with same power).

✓ Use "FOIL". (First-Out-In-Last) for binomials:

$$(x + a)(x + b) = x^2 + (b + a)x + ab$$

✓ Add or Subtract "like" terms using order of operation.

*Example:*

1) Simplify this expression. $4x(6x - 3) =$

Use Distributive Property: $4x(6x - 3) = 24x^2 - 12x$

2) Simplify this expression. $(6x - 2)(2x - 3) =$

First apply FOIL method: $(a + b)(c + d) = ac + ad + bc + bd$

$(6x - 2)(2x - 3) = 12x^2 - 18x - 4x + 6$

Now combine like terms: $12x^2 - 18x - 4x + 6 = 12x^2 - 22x + 6$

## ✍ *Simplify each expression.*

1) $5(2x - 10) =$

2) $2x(4x - 2) =$

3) $4x(5x - 3) =$

4) $3x(7x + 3) =$

5) $4x(8x - 4) =$

6) $5x(5x + 4) =$

7) $(2x - 3)(x - 4) =$

8) $(x - 5)(3x + 4) =$

9) $(x - 5)(x - 3) =$

10) $(3x + 8)(3x - 8) =$

11) $(3x - 8)(3x - 4) =$

12) $3x^2 + 3x^2 - 2x^3 =$

# Adding and Subtracting Polynomials

**Step-by-step guide:**

- ✓ Adding polynomials is just a matter of combining like terms, with some order of operations considerations thrown in.
- ✓ Be careful with the minus signs, and don't confuse addition and multiplication!

## *Example:*

1) Simplify the expressions. $(4x^3 + 3x^4) - (x^4 - 5x^3) =$

First use Distributive Property for $-(x^4 - 5x^3)$, $\rightarrow -(x^4 - 5x^3) = -x^4 + 5x^3$

$(4x^3 + 3x^4) - (x^4 - 5x^3) = 4x^3 + 3x^4 - x^4 + 5x^3$

Now combine like terms: $4x^3 + 3x^4 - x^4 + 5x^3 = 2x^4 + 9x^3$

2) Add expressions. $(2x^3 - 6) + (9x^3 - 4x^2) =$

Remove parentheses: $(2x^3 - 6) + (9x^3 - 4x^2) = 2x^3 - 6 + 9x^3 - 4x^2$

Now combine like terms: $2x^3 - 6 + 9x^3 - 4x^2 = 11x^3 - 4x^2 - 6$

## ✍ *Add or subtract expressions.*

1) $(-x^2 - 2) + (2x^2 + 1) =$

2) $(2x^2 + 3) - (3 - 4x^2) =$

3) $(2x^3 + 3x^2) - (x^3 + 8) =$

4) $(4x^3 - x^2) + (3x^2 - 5x) =$

5) $(7x^3 + 9x) - (3x^3 + 2) =$

6) $(2x^3 - 2) + (2x^3 + 2) =$

7) $(4x^3 + 5) - (7 - 2x^3) =$

8) $(4x^2 + 2x^3) - (2x^3 + 5) =$

9) $(4x^2 - x) + (3x - 5x^2) =$

10) $(7x + 9) - (3x + 9) =$

11) $(4x^4 - 2x) - (6x - 2x^4) =$

12) $(12x - 4x^3) - (8x^3 + 6x) =$

# Answers – Day 20

## Writing Polynomials in Standard Form

1) $2x$

2) $-3$

3) $-5x^3 + 3x^2$

4) $4x^3$

5) $-6x^3 + 2x^2 + x$

6) $2x^3 - x^2$

7) $4x^3 - 2x^2 + 2x$

8) $-6x^3 - 2x^2 + 4x$

9) $2x^2 - 5x + 2$

10) $9x^4 - 7x + 12$

11) $-2x^3 + 5x^2 + 13x$

12) $-x^3 + 6x^2 + 10$

## Simplifying Polynomials

1) $10x - 50$

2) $8x^2 - 4x$

3) $20x^2 - 12x$

4) $21x^2 + 9x$

5) $32x^2 - 16x$

6) $25x^2 + 20x$

7) $2x^2 - 11x + 12$

8) $3x^2 - 11x - 20$

9) $x^2 - 8x + 15$

10) $9x^2 - 64$

11) $9x^2 - 36x + 32$

12) $-2x^3 + 6x^2$

## Adding and Subtracting Polynomials

1) $x^2 - 1$

2) $6x^2$

3) $x^3 + 3x^2 - 8$

4) $4x^3 + 2x^2 - 5x$

5) $4x^3 + 9x - 2$

6) $4x^3$

7) $6x^3 - 2$

8) $4x^2 - 5$

9) $-x^2 + 2x$

10) $4x$

11) $6x^4 - 8x$

12) $-12x^3 + 6x$

# Day 21: Monomials Operations

**Math Topics that you'll learn today:**

- ✓ Multiplying Monomials

- ✓ Multiplying and Dividing Monomials

- ✓ Multiplying a Polynomial and a Monomial

# Multiplying Monomials

**Step-by-step guide:**

    ✓ A monomial is a polynomial with just one term, like $2x$ or $7y$.

***Example:***

1) Multiply expressions. $5a^4b^3 \times 2a^3b^2 =$

Use this formula: $x^a \times x^b = x^{a+b}$

$a^4 \times a^3 = a^{4+3} = a^7$ and $b^3 \times b^2 = b^{3+2} = b^5$

Then: $5a^4b^3 \times 2a^3b^2 = 10a^7b^5$

2) Multiply expressions. $-4xy^4z^2 \times 3x^2y^5z^3 =$

Use this formula: $x^a \times x^b = x^{a+b}$

$x \times x^2 = x^{1+2} = x^3$ , $y^4 \times y^5 = y^{4+5} = y^9$ and $z^2 \times z^3 = z^{2+3} = z^5$

Then: $-4xy^4z^2 \times 3x^2y^5z^3 = -12x^3y^9z^5$

## ✍ *Simplify each expression.*

1) $4u^9 \times (-2u^3) =$

2) $(-2p^7) \times (-3p^2) =$

3) $3xy^2z^3 \times 2z^2 =$

4) $5u^5t \times 3ut^2 =$

5) $(-9a^6) \times (-5a^2b^4) =$

6) $-2a^3b^2 \times 4a^2b =$

7) $2xy^2 \times x^2y^3 =$

8) $3p^2q^4 \times (-2pq^3) =$

9) $4s^5t^2 \times 4st^3 =$

10) $(-6x^3y^2) \times 3x^2y =$

11) $2xy^2z \times 4z^2 =$

12) $4xy \times x^2y =$

# Multiplying and Dividing Monomials

**Step-by-step guide:**

✓ When you divide two monomials you need to divide their coefficients and then divide their variables.

✓ In case of exponents with the same base, you need to subtract their powers.

✓ Exponent's rules:

$$x^a \times x^b = x^{a+b}, \qquad \frac{x^a}{x^b} = x^{a-b}$$
$$\frac{1}{x^b} = x^{-b}, \quad (x^a)^b = x^{a \times b}$$
$$(xy)^a = x^a \times y^a$$

***Example:***

1) Multiply expressions. $(-3x^7)(4x^3) =$

Use this formula: $x^a \times x^b = x^{a+b} \rightarrow x^7 \times x^3 = x^{10}$

Then: $(-3x^7)(4x^3) = -12x^{10}$

2) Dividing expressions. $\frac{18x^2y^5}{2xy^4} =$

Use this formula: $\frac{x^a}{x^b} = x^{a-b}$, $\frac{x^2}{x} = x^{2-1} = x$ and $\frac{y^5}{y^4} = y^{5-4} = y$

Then: $\frac{18x^2y^5}{2xy^4} = 9xy$

✎ ***Simplify each expression.***

1) $(-2x^3y^4)(3x^3y^2) =$

2) $(-5x^3y^2)(-2x^4y^5) =$

3) $(9x^5y)(-3x^3y^3) =$

4) $(8x^7y^2)(6x^5y^4) =$

5) $(7x^4y^6)(4x^3y^4) =$

6) $(12x^2y^9)(7x^9y^{12}) =$

7) $\frac{12x^6y^8}{4x^4y^2} =$

8) $\frac{26x^9y^5}{2x^3y^4} =$

9) $\frac{80x^{12}y^9}{10x^6y^7} =$

10) $\frac{95x^{18}y^7}{5x^9y^2} =$

11) $\frac{200x^3y^8}{40x^3y^7} =$

12) $\frac{-15x^{17}y^{13}}{3x^6y^9} =$

# Multiplying a Polynomial and a Monomial

**Step-by-step guide:**

✓ When multiplying monomials, use the product rule for exponents.

✓ When multiplying a monomial by a polynomial, use the distributive property.

$$a \times (b + c) = a \times b + a \times c$$

*Example:*

1) Multiply expressions. $-4x(5x + 9) =$

Use Distributive Property: $-4x(5x + 9) = -20x^2 - 36x$

2) Multiply expressions. $2x(6x^2 - 3y^2) =$

Use Distributive Property: $2x(6x^2 - 3y^2) = 12x^3 - 6xy^2$

✎ *Find each product.*

1) $3x(9x + 2y) =$

2) $6x(x + 2y) =$

3) $9x(2x + 4y) =$

4) $12x(3x + 9) =$

5) $11x(2x - 11y) =$

6) $2x(6x - 6y) =$

7) $2x(3x - 6y + 3) =$

8) $5x(3x^2 + 2y^2) =$

9) $13x(4x + 8y) =$

10) $5(2x^2 - 9y^2) =$

11) $3x(-2x^2y + 3y) =$

12) $-2(2x^2 - 2xy + 2) =$

# Answers – Day 21

## Multiplying Monomials

1) $-8u^{12}$

2) $6p^9$

3) $6xy^2z^5$

4) $15u^6t^3$

5) $45a^8b^4$

6) $-8a^5b^3$

7) $2x^3y^5$

8) $-6p^3q^7$

9) $16s^6t^5$

10) $-18x^5y^3$

11) $8xy^2z^3$

12) $4x^3y^2$

## Multiplying and Dividing Monomials

1) $-6x^6y^6$

2) $10x^7y^7$

3) $-27x^8y^4$

4) $48x^{12}y^6$

5) $28x^7y^{10}$

6) $84x^{11}y^{21}$

7) $3x^2y^6$

8) $13x^6y$

9) $8x^6y^2$

10) $19x^9y^5$

11) $5y$

12) $-5x^{11}y^4$

## Multiplying a Polynomial and a Monomial

1) $27x^2 + 6xy$

2) $6x^2 + 12xy$

3) $18x^2 + 36xy$

4) $36x^2 + 108x$

5) $22x^2 - 121xy$

6) $12x^2 - 12xy$

7) $6x^2 - 12xy + 6x$

8) $15x^3 + 10xy^2$

9) $52x^2 + 104xy$

10) $10x^2 - 45y^2$

11) $-6x^3y + 9xy$

12) $-4x^2 + 4xy - 4$

# Day 22: Polynomials Operations

**Math Topics that you'll learn today:**

- ✓ Multiplying Binomials

- ✓ Factoring Trinomials

- ✓ Operations with Polynomials

*Mathematics compares the most diverse phenomena and discovers the secret analogies that unite them. – Joseph Fourier*

# Multiplying Binomials

**Step-by-step guide:**

✓ Use "FOIL". (First–Out–In–Last)
$$(x + a)(x + b) = x^2 + (b + a)x + ab$$

*Example:*

1) Multiply Binomials. $(x - 2)(x + 2) =$

Use "FOIL". (First–Out–In–Last): $(x - 2)(x + 2) = x^2 + 2x - 2x - 4$

Then simplify: $x^2 + 2x - 2x - 4 = x^2 - 4$

2) Multiply Binomials. $(x + 5)(x - 2) =$

Use "FOIL". (First–Out–In–Last):

$(x + 5)(x - 2) = x^2 - 2x + 5x - 10$

Then simplify: $x^2 - 2x + 5x - 10 = x^2 + 3x - 10$

✎ *Find each product.*

1) $(x + 2)(x + 2) =$

2) $(x - 3)(x + 2) =$

3) $(x - 2)(x - 4) =$

4) $(x + 3)(x + 2) =$

5) $(x - 4)(x - 5) =$

6) $(x + 5)(x + 2) =$

7) $(x - 6)(x + 3) =$

8) $(x - 8)(x - 4) =$

9) $(x + 2)(x + 8) =$

10) $(x - 2)(x + 4) =$

11) $(x + 4)(x + 4) =$

12) $(x + 5)(x + 5) =$

# Factoring Trinomials

**Step-by-step guide:**

- ✓ "FOIL":
$$(x + a)(x + b) = x^2 + (b + a)x + ab$$
- ✓ "Difference of Squares":
$$a^2 - b^2 = (a + b)(a - b)$$
$$a^2 + 2ab + b^2 = (a + b)(a + b)$$
$$a^2 - 2ab + b^2 = (a - b)(a - b)$$
- ✓ "Reverse FOIL":
$$x^2 + (b + a)x + ab = (x + a)(x + b)$$

*Example:*

1) Factor this trinomial. $x^2 - 2x - 8 =$
   Break the expression into groups: $(x^2 + 2x) + (-4x - 8)$
   Now factor out $x$ from $x^2 + 2x$ : $x(x + 2)$ and factor out $-4$ from $-4x - 8$: $-4(x + 2)$
   Then: $= x(x + 2) - 4(x + 2)$ , now factor out like term: $x + 2$
   Then: $(x + 2)(x - 4)$

2) Factor this trinomial. $x^2 - 6x + 8 =$
   Break the expression into groups: $(x^2 - 2x) + (-4x + 8)$
   Now factor out $x$ from $x^2 - 2x$ : $x(x - 2)$ , and factor out $-4$ from $-4x + 8$: $-4(x - 2)$
   Then: $= x(x - 2) - 4(x - 2)$ , now factor out like term: $x - 2$
   Then: $(x - 2)(x - 4)$

✎ *Factor each trinomial.*

1) $x^2 + 8x + 15 =$

2) $x^2 - 5x + 6 =$

3) $x^2 + 6x + 8 =$

4) $x^2 - 8x + 16 =$

5) $x^2 - 7x + 12 =$

6) $x^2 + 11x + 18 =$

7) $x^2 + 2x - 24 =$

8) $x^2 + 4x - 12 =$

9) $x^2 - 10x + 9 =$

10) $x^2 + 5x - 14 =$

11) $x^2 - 6x - 27 =$

12) $x^2 - 11x - 42 =$

# Operations with Polynomials

**Step-by-step guide:**

✓ When multiplying a monomial by a polynomial, use the distributive property.

$$a \times (b + c) = a \times b + a \times c$$

*Example:*

1) Multiply. $5(2x - 6) =$

Use the distributive property: $5(2x - 6) = 10x - 30$

2) Multiply. $2x(6x + 2) =$

Use the distributive property: $2x(6 + 2) = 12x^2 + 4x$

✏ *Find each product.*

1) $9(6x + 2) =$                         7) $6x^3(-3x + 4) =$

2) $8(3x + 7) =$                         8) $-7x^4(2x - 4) =$

3) $5(6x - 1) =$                         9) $8(x^2 + 2x - 3) =$

4) $-3(8x - 3) =$                       10) $4(4x^2 - 2x + 1) =$

5) $3x^2(6x - 5) =$                      11) $2(3x^2 + 2x - 2) =$

6) $5x^2(7x - 2) =$                      12) $8x(5x^2 + 3x + 8) =$

# Answers – Day 22

## Multiplying Binomials

1) $x^2 + 4x + 4$

2) $x^2 - x - 6$

3) $x^2 - 6x + 8$

4) $x^2 + 5x + 6$

5) $x^2 - 9x + 20$

6) $x^2 + 7x + 10$

7) $x^2 - 3x - 18$

8) $x^2 - 12x + 32$

9) $x^2 + 10x + 16$

10) $x^2 + 2x - 8$

11) $x^2 + 8x + 16$

12) $x^2 + 10x + 25$

## Factoring Trinomials

1) $(x + 3)(x + 5)$

2) $(x - 2)(x - 3)$

3) $(x + 4)(x + 2)$

4) $(x - 4)(x - 4)$

5) $(x - 3)(x - 4)$

6) $(x + 2)(x + 9)$

7) $(x + 6)(x - 4)$

8) $(x - 2)(x + 6)$

9) $(x - 1)(x - 9)$

10) $(x - 2)(x + 7)$

11) $(x - 9)(x + 3)$

12) $(x + 3)(x - 14)$

## Operations with Polynomials

1) $54x + 18$

2) $24x + 56$

3) $30x - 5$

4) $-24x + 9$

5) $18x^3 - 15x^2$

6) $35x^3 - 10x^2$

7) $-18x^4 + 24x^3$

8) $-14x^5 + 28x^4$

9) $8x^2 + 16x - 24$

10) $16x^2 - 8x + 4$

11) $6x^2 + 4x - 4$

12) $40x^3 + 24x^2 + 64x$

# Day 23: System of Equations

## Math Topics that you'll learn today:

- ✓ Solving Systems of Equations

- ✓ Systems of Equations Word Problems

*Mathematics is a hard thing to love. It has the unfortunate habit, like a rude dog, of turning its most unfavorable side towards you when you first make contact with it. ~ David Whiteland*

# Systems of Equations

**Step-by-step guide:**

✓ A system of equations contains two equations and two variables. For example, consider the system of equations: $x - y = 1, x + y = 5$

✓ The easiest way to solve a system of equation is using the elimination method. The elimination method uses the addition property of equality. You can add the same value to each side of an equation.

✓ For the first equation above, you can add $x + y$ to the left side and 5 to the right side of the first equation: $x - y + (x + y) = 1 + 5$. Now, if you simplify, you get: $x - y + (x + y) = 1 + 5 \rightarrow 2x = 6 \rightarrow x = 3$. Now, substitute 3 for the $x$ in the first equation: $3 - y = 1$. By solving this equation, $y = 2$

**Example:**

What is the value of $x + y$ in this system of equations? $\begin{cases} 3x - 4y = -20 \\ -x + 2y = 10 \end{cases}$

Solving Systems of Equations by Elimination: $\dfrac{\begin{aligned} 3x - 4y &= -20 \\ -x + 2y &= 10 \end{aligned}}{}$ ⇒ Multiply the second

equation by 3, then add it to the first equation.

$\begin{aligned} 3x - 4y &= -20 \\ 3(-x + 2y &= 10) \end{aligned} \Rightarrow \begin{aligned} 3x - 4y &= -20 \\ -3x + 6y &= 30) \end{aligned} \Rightarrow 2y = 10 \Rightarrow y = 5$. Now, substitute 5 for $y$ in the

first equation and solve for $x$. $3x - 4(5) = -20 \rightarrow 3x - 20 = -20 \rightarrow x = 0$

Thus, $x + y = 0 + 5 = 5$

## ✍ *Solve each system of equations.*

1) $-2x + 2y = 4$        $x = \underline{\quad}$

$-2x + y = 3$        $y = \underline{\quad}$

2) $-10x + 2y = -6$        $x = \underline{\quad}$

$6x - 16y = 48$        $y = \underline{\quad}$

3) $y = -8$        $x = \underline{\quad}$

$16x - 12y = 32$

4) $2y = -6x + 10$        $x = \underline{\quad}$

$10x - 8y = -6$        $y = \underline{\quad}$

5) $10x - 9y = -13$        $x = \underline{\quad}$

$-5x + 3y = 11$        $y = \underline{\quad}$

6) $-3x - 4y = 5$        $x = \underline{\quad}$

$x - 2y = 5$        $y = \underline{\quad}$

# Systems of Equations Word Problems

**Step-by-step guide:**

✓ Define your variables, write two equations, and use elimination method for solving systems of equations.

**Example:**

Tickets to a movie cost $8 for adults and $5 for students. A group of friends purchased 20 tickets for $115.00. How many adults ticket did they buy? ____

Let $x$ be the number of adult tickets and $y$ be the number of student tickets. There are 20 tickets. Then: $x + y = 20$. The cost of adults' tickets is $8 and for students it is $5, and the total cost is $115. So, $8x + 5y = 20$. Now, we have a system of equations: $\begin{cases} x + y = 20 \\ 8x + 5y = 115 \end{cases}$

Multiply the first equation by $-5$ and add to the second equation: $-5(x + y = 20) = -5x - 5y = -100$

$8x + 5y + (-5x - 5y) = 115 - 100 \rightarrow 3x = 15 \rightarrow x = 5 \rightarrow 5 + y = 20 \rightarrow y = 15$. There are 5 adult tickets and 15 student tickets.

✎ *Solve each word problem.*

1) Tickets to a movie cost $5 for adults and $3 for students. A group of friends purchased **18** tickets for $**82.00**. How many adults ticket did they buy? _____

2) At a store, Eva bought two shirts and five hats for $**154.00**. Nicole bought three same shirts and four same hats for $**168.00**. What is the price of each shirt? _____

3) A farmhouse shelters **10** animals, some are pigs, and some are ducks. Altogether there are **36** legs. How many pigs are there? _____

4) A class of **195** students went on a field trip. They took **19** vehicles, some cars and some buses. If each car holds **5** students and each bus hold **25** students, how many buses did they take? _____

# Answers – Day 23

### Systems of Equations

1) $x = -1, y = 1$

2) $x = 0, y = -3$

3) $x = -4$

4) $x = 1, y = 2$

5) $x = -4, y = -3$

6) $x = 1, y = -2$

### Systems of Equations Word Problems

1)  14

2)  $32

3)  8

4)  5

# Day 24: Triangles and Polygons

## Math Topics that you'll learn today:

- ✓ The Pythagorean Theorem

- ✓ Triangles

- ✓ Polygons

*Mathematics is like checkers in being suitable for the young, not too difficult, amusing, and without peril to the state. – Plato*

# The Pythagorean Theorem

**Step-by-step guide:**

    ✓ In any right triangle: $a^2 + b^2 = c^2$

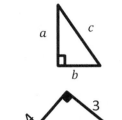

***Example:***

1) Find the missing length.

    Use Pythagorean Theorem: $a^2 + b^2 = c^2$

    Then: $a^2 + b^2 = c^2 \rightarrow 3^2 + 4^2 = c^2 \rightarrow 9 + 16 = c^2$

    $c^2 = 25 \rightarrow c = 5$

2) Right triangle ABC has two legs of lengths 6 cm (AB) and 8 cm (AC). What is the length of the third side (BC)?

    Use Pythagorean Theorem: $a^2 + b^2 = c^2$

    Then: $a^2 + b^2 = c^2 \rightarrow 6^2 + 8^2 = c^2 \rightarrow 36 + 64 = c^2$

    $c^2 = 100 \rightarrow c = 10$

 ***Find the missing side.***

| 1) | 2) | 3) | 4) |
|---|---|---|---|
|  | | | |

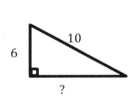

| 5) | 6) | 7) | 8) |
|---|---|---|---|

 www.EffortlessMath.com

# Triangles

### Step-by-step guide:

✓ In any triangle the sum of all angles is **180** degrees.
✓ Area of a triangle = $\frac{1}{2}$ ($base \times height$)

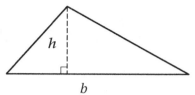

### *Example:*

What is the area of triangles?

1)

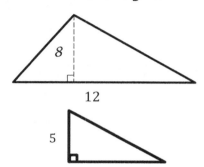

**Solution:**

Use the are formula: Area $= \frac{1}{2}$ ($base \times height$)
$base = 12$ and $height = 8$
Area $= \frac{1}{2}(12 \times 8) = \frac{1}{2}(96) = 48$

2)

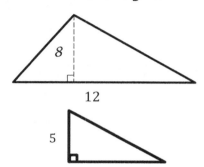

**Solution:**

Use the are formula: Area $= \frac{1}{2}$ ($base \times height$)
$base = 6$ and $height = 5$
Area $= \frac{1}{2}(5 \times 6) = \frac{30}{2} = 15$

✎ *Find the measure of the unknown angle in each triangle.*

1)

70°
95°
?°

2)

60°
85°
?°

3)

80°
85°
?°

4)

50°
65°
?°

✎ *Find area of each triangle.*

5)

10
6
8

6)

13
12
5

7)

14 cm
8 cm
16 cm

8)

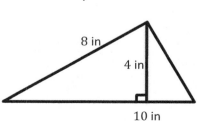

8 in
4 in
10 in

# Polygons

### Step-by-step guide:

| | |
|---|---|
| Perimeter of a square $= 4 \times side = 4s$ | Perimeter of a rectangle $= 2(width + length)$ |
| Perimeter of trapezoid $= a + b + c + d$ | Perimeter of a regular hexagon $= 6a$ |
| **Example:** Find the perimeter of following regular hexagon. Perimeter of Pentagon $= 6a$ Perimeter of Pentagon $= 6a = 6 \times 3 = 18m$ | Perimeter of a parallelogram $= 2(l + w)$ |

✎ *Find the perimeter of each shape.*

1)
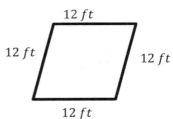
12 ft
12 ft   12 ft
12 ft

2)

10 in
8 in        8 in
10 in

3)
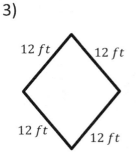
12 ft   12 ft
12 ft   12 ft

4) Square

14 cm

5) Regular hexagon

5 m

6)
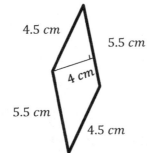
4.5 cm
5.5 cm
4 cm
5.5 cm
4.5 cm

7) Parallelogram
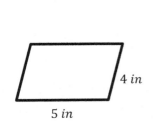
4 in
5 in

8) Square

6 m

# Answers – Day 24

### *The Pythagorean Theorem*

1) 5

2) 17

3) 15

4) 8

5) 5

6) 30

7) 30

8) 12

### *Triangles*

1) 15°

2) 35°

3) 15°

4) 65°

5) 24 square unites

6) 30 square unites

7) 64 square unites

8) 20 square unites

### *Polygons*

1) 48 $ft$

2) 36 $in$

3) 48 $ft$

4) 56 $cm$

5) 30 $m$

6) 20 $cm$

7) 18 $in$

8) 24 $m$

# Day 25: Circles, Trapezoids and Cubes

**Math Topics that you'll learn today:**

- ✓ Circles

- ✓ Trapezoids

- ✓ Cubes

*Mathematics is as much an aspect of culture as it is a collection of algorithms. – Carl Boyer*

# Circles

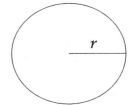

### Step-by-step guide:

- ✓ In a circle, variable $r$ is usually used for the radius and $d$ for diameter and $\pi$ is about **3.14**.
- ✓ Area of a circle $= \pi r^2$
- ✓ Circumference of a circle $= 2\pi r$

**Example:**

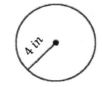

1) Find the area of the circle.

   Use area formula: $Area = \pi r^2$ ,

   $r = 4$ then: Area $= \pi(4)^2 = 16\pi$, $\pi = 3.14$ then: Area $= 16 \times 3.14 = 50.24$

2) Find the Circumference of the circle.

   Use Circumference formula: Circumference $= 2\pi r$

   $r = 6$ , then: Circumference $= 2\pi(6) = 12\pi$

   $\pi = 3.14$ then: Circumference $= 12 \times 3.14 = 37.68$

✎ **Complete the table below.** ($\pi = 3.14$)

|  | Radius | Diameter | Circumference | Area |
|---|---|---|---|---|
| **Circle 1** | 4 inches | 8 inches | 25.12 inches | 50.24 square inches |
| **Circle 2** |  | 12 meters |  |  |
| **Circle 3** |  |  |  | 12.56 square ft |
| **Circle 4** |  |  | 18.84 miles |  |
| **Circle 5** |  | 5 kilometers |  |  |
| **Circle 6** | 6 centimeters |  |  |  |
| **Circle 7** |  | 8 feet |  |  |
| **Circle 8** |  |  |  | 28.26 square meters |

# Trapezoids

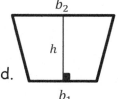

**Step-by-step guide:**

✓ A quadrilateral with at least one pair of parallel sides is a trapezoid.
✓ Area of a trapezoid $= \frac{1}{2}h(b_1 + b_2)$

**Example:**

Calculate the area of the trapezoid.

Use area formula: $A = \frac{1}{2}h(b_1 + b_2)$

$b_1 = 12$ , $b_2 = 16$ and $h = 18$

Then: $A = \frac{1}{2}18(12 + 16) = 9(28) = 252 \; cm^2$

✎ *Find the area of each trapezoid.*

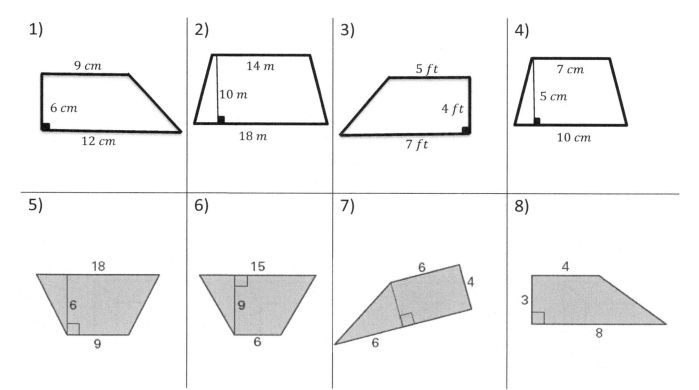

1)

2)

3)

4)

5)

6)

7)

8)

# Cubes

## Step-by-step guide:

✓ A cube is a three-dimensional solid object bounded by six square sides.
✓ Volume is the measure of the amount of space inside of a solid figure, like a cube, ball, cylinder or pyramid.
✓ Volume of a cube = $(one\ side)^3$
✓ surface area of cube = $6 \times (one\ side)^2$

**Example:**

Find the volume and surface area of this cube.

Use volume formula: $volume = (one\ side)^3$

Then: $volume = (one\ side)^3 = (2)^3 = 8\ cm^3$

Use surface area formula:

surface area of cube: $6(one\ side)^2 = 6(2)^2 = 6(4) = 24\ cm^2$

2 cm

✏️ *Find the volume of each cube.*

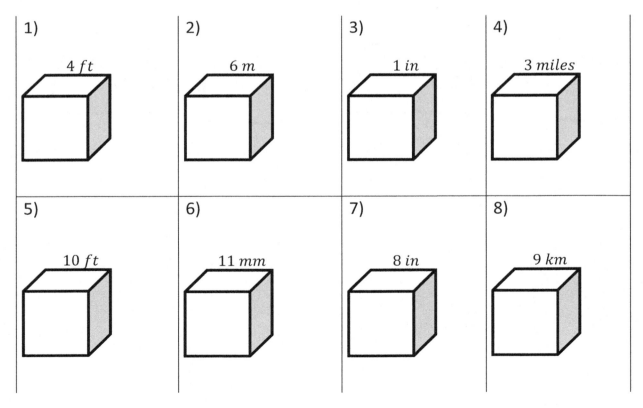

1) 4 ft

2) 6 m

3) 1 in

4) 3 miles

5) 10 ft

6) 11 mm

7) 8 in

8) 9 km

# Answers – Day 25

### Circles

|  | Radius | Diameter | Circumference | Area |
|---|---|---|---|---|
| Circle 1 | 4 inches | 8 inches | 25.12 inches | 50.24 square inches |
| Circle 2 | 6 meters | 12 meters | 37.68 meters | 113.04 meters |
| Circle 3 | 2 square ft | 4 square ft | 12.56 square ft | 12.56 square ft |
| Circle 4 | 3 miles | 6 miles | 18.84 miles | 28.26 miles |
| Circle 5 | 2.5 kilometers | 5 kilometers | 15.7 kilometers | 19.625 kilometers |
| Circle 6 | 6 centimeters | 12 centimeters | 37.68 centimeters | 113.04 centimeters |
| Circle 7 | 4 feet | 8 feet | 25.12 feet | 50.24 feet |
| Circle 8 | 3 square meters | 6 square meters | 18.84 square meters | 28.26 square meters |

### Trapezoids

1) $63\ cm^2$

2) $160\ m^2$

3) $24\ ft^2$

4) $42.5\ cm^2$

5) 81

6) 94.5

7) 36

8) 18

### Cubes

1) $64\ ft^3$

2) $216\ m^3$

3) $1\ in^3$

4) $27\ miles^3$

5) $1,000\ ft^3$

6) $1,331\ mm^3$

7) $512\ in^3$

8) $729\ km^3$

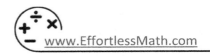

www.EffortlessMath.com

# Day 26: Rectangular Prisms and Cylinder

## Math Topics that you'll learn today:

✓ Rectangle Prisms

✓ Cylinder

*It's fine to work on any problem, so long as it generates interesting mathematics along the way – even if you don't solve it at the end of the day." – Andrew Wiles*

# Rectangular Prisms

**Step-by-step guide:**

- ✓ A solid 3-dimensional object which has six rectangular faces.
- ✓ Volume of a Rectangular prism = **Length × Width × Height**

Volume = $l \times w \times h$    Surface area = $2(wh + lw + lh)$

**Example:**

Find the volume and surface area of rectangular prism.

Use volume formula: $Volume = l \times w \times h$

Then: $Volume = 10 \times 5 \times 8 = 400 \ m^3$

Use surface area formula: $Surface\ area = 2(wh + lw + lh)$

Then: $Surface\ area = 2(5 \times 8 + 10 \times 5 + 10 \times 8) = 2(40 + 50 + 80) = 340 \ m^2$

✍ *Find the volume of each Rectangular Prism.*

1)

7 m  6 m  5 m

2)

10 in  8 in  4 in

3)

9 m  7 m  3 m

4)

3 cm  5 cm  10 cm

5)

6 ft  12 ft  8 ft

6)

6 m  8 m  5 m

# Cylinder

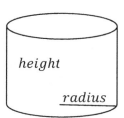

## Step-by-step guide:

✓ A cylinder is a solid geometric figure with straight parallel sides and a circular or oval cross section.
✓ Volume of Cylinder Formula = $\pi(radius)^2 \times height$  $\pi = 3.14$
✓ Surface area of a cylinder = $2\pi r^2 + 2\pi rh$

*height*

*radius*

**Example:**

Find the volume and Surface area of the follow Cylinder.

6 *cm*

4 *cm*

Use volume formula: $Volume = \pi(radius)^2 \times height$
Then:  $Volume = \pi(4)^2 \times 6 = \pi 16 \times 6 = 96\pi$
$\pi = 3.14$ then: $Volume = 96\pi = 301.44$
Use surface area formula: $Surface\ area = 2\pi r^2 + 2\pi rh$
Then:  $= 2\pi(4)^2 + 2\pi(4)(6) = 2\pi(16) + 2\pi(24) = 32\pi + 48\pi = 80\pi$
$\pi = 3.14$ then: $Surface\ area = 80 \times 3.14 = 251.2$

✎ *Find the volume of each Cylinder. Round your answer to the nearest tenth.* ($\pi = 3.14$)

| | | |
|---|---|---|
| 1) | 2) | 3) |

8 m

10m

2 cm

4cm

6 cm

5 cm

| | | |
|---|---|---|
| 4) | 5) | 6) |

7.6 m

14.2 m

8 m

6 m

6 in

4 in

# Answers – Day 26

### *Rectangle Prisms*

1) $210\ m^3$

2) $320\ in^3$

3) $189\ m^3$

4) $150\ cm^3$

5) $576\ ft^3$

6) $240\ m^3$

### *Cylinder*

1) $2{,}009.6\ m^3$

2) $50.24\ cm^3$

3) $565.2\ cm^3$

4) $2{,}575.4\ m^3$

5) $904.3\ m^3$

6) $301.4\ in^3$

# Day 27: Statistics

**Math Topics that you'll learn today:**

- ✓ Mean, Median, Mode, and Range of the Given Data

- ✓ Histograms

- ✓ Pie Graph

- ✓ Probability Problems

*"Millions saw the apple fall, but Newton asked why." – Bernard Baruch*

# Mean, Median, Mode, and Range of the Given Data

**Step-by-step guide:**

- ✓ Mean: $\dfrac{sum\ of\ the\ data}{total\ number\ of\ data\ entires}$
- ✓ Mode: value in the list that appears most often
- ✓ Range: the difference of largest value and smallest value in the list

## *Example:*

1) What is the median of these numbers? $4, 9, 13, 8, 15, 18, 5$

   Write the numbers in order: $4, 5, 8, 9, 13, 15, 18$

   Median is the number in the middle. Therefore, the median is 9.

2) What is the mode of these numbers? $22, 16, 12, 9, 7, 6, 4, 6$

   Mode: value in the list that appears most often
   Therefore, mode is 6.

## ✍ Solve.

1) In a javelin throw competition, five athletics score $56, 58, 63, 57$ and $61$ meters. What are their Mean and Median? _____

2) Eva went to shop and bought 3 apples, 5 peaches, 8 bananas, 1 pineapple and 3 melons. What are the Mean and Median of her purchase? _____

## ✍ *Find Mode and Rage of the Given Data.*

3) $8, 2, 5, 9, 1, 2$

Mode: _____　　　　Range: _____

4) $4, 4, 3, 9, 7, 9, 4, 6, 4$

Mode: _____　　　　Range: _____

5) $6, 6, 2, 3, 6, 3, 9, 12$

Mode: _____　　　　Range: _____

6) $12, 9, 2, 9, 3, 2, 9, 5$

Mode: _____　　　　Range: _____

# Histograms

**Step-by-step guide:**

✓ A histogram is an accurate representation of the distribution of numerical data.

**Example:**

*Use the following Graph to complete the table.*

| Day | Distance (km) |
|-----|---------------|
| 1 | |
| 2 | |
| | |
| | |
| | |

→

Answer:

| Day | Distance (km) |
|-----|---------------|
| 1 | 359 |
| 2 | 460 |
| 3 | 278 |
| 4 | 547 |
| 5 | 360 |

✍ The following table shows the number of births in the US from 2007 to 2012 (in millions).

| Year | Number of births (in millions) |
|------|-------------------------------|
| 2007 | 4.32 |
| 2008 | 4.25 |
| 2009 | 4.13 |
| 2010 | 4 |
| 2011 | 3.95 |
| 2012 | 3.95 |

Draw a histogram for the table.

# Pie Graph

**Step-by-step guide:**

✓ **A Pie Chart is a circle chart divided into sectors, each sector represents the relative size of each value.**

*Example:*

A library has 840 books that include Mathematics, Physics, Chemistry, English and History. Use following graph to answer question.

What is the number of Mathematics books?

Number of total books $= 840$,
Percent of Mathematics books $= 30\% = 0.30$
Then: $0.30 \times 840 = 252$

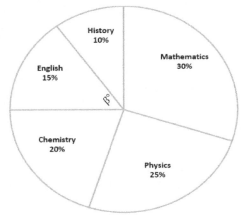

✎ **The circle graph below shows all Jason's expenses for last month. Jason spent $300 on his bills last month.**

1) How much did Jason spend on his car last month? _____

2) How much did Jason spend for foods last month? _____

3) How much did Jason spend on his rent last month? _____

4) What fraction is Jason's expenses for his bills and Car out of his total expenses last month?

Jason's monthly expenses

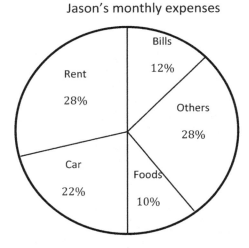

# Probability Problems

**Step-by-step guide:**

- ✓ Probability is the likelihood of something happening in the future. It is expressed as a number between zero (can never happen) to 1 (will always happen).
- ✓ Probability can be expressed as a fraction, a decimal, or a percent.

### *Example:*

1) If there are 8 red balls and 12 blue balls in a basket, what is the probability that John will pick out a red ball from the basket?

There are 8 red ball and 20 are total number of balls. Therefore, probability that John will pick out a red ball from the basket is 8 out of 20 or $\frac{8}{8+12} = \frac{8}{20} = \frac{2}{5}$.

2) A bag contains 18 balls: two green, five black, eight blue, a brown, a red and one white. If 17 balls are removed from the bag at random, what is the probability that a brown ball has been removed?

If 17 balls are removed from the bag at random, there will be one ball in the bag.
The probability of choosing a brown ball is 1 out of 18. Therefore, the probability of not choosing a brown ball is 17 out of 18 and the probability of having not a brown ball after removing 17 balls is the same.

## ✎ *Solve.*

1) A number is chosen at random from 1 to 10. Find the probability of selecting number 4 or smaller numbers. _____

2) Bag A contains 9 red marbles and 3 green marbles. Bag B contains 9 black marbles and 6 orange marbles. What is the probability of selecting a green marble at random from bag A? What is the probability of selecting a black marble at random from Bag B? _____

# Answers – Day 27

### Mean, Median, Mode, and Range of the Given Data

1) Mean: 59, Median: 58

2) Mean: 4, Median: 3

3) Mode: 2, Range: 8

4) Mode: 6, Range: 6

5) Mode: 6, Range: 10

6) Mode: 9, Range: 10

### Histograms

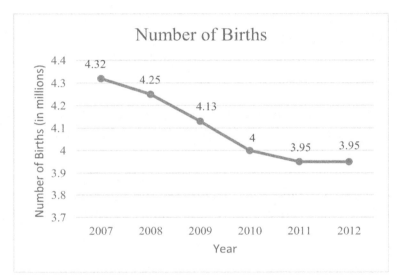

### Pie Graph

1) $550
2) $250
3) $700
4) $\frac{17}{50}$

### Probability Problems

1) $\frac{2}{5}$

2) $\frac{1}{4}, \frac{3}{5}$

# Day 28: Functions

## Math Topics that you'll learn today:

- ✓ Function Notation
- ✓ Adding and Subtracting Functions
- ✓ Multiplying and Dividing Functions
- ✓ Composition of Functions

*Mathematics is the supreme judge; from its decisions there is no appeal.*

*– Tobias Dantzig*

## Function Notation

**Step-by-step guide:**

- ✓ Functions are mathematical operations that assign unique outputs to given inputs.
- ✓ Function notation is the way a function is written. It is meant to be a precise way of giving information about the function without a rather lengthy written explanation.
- ✓ The most popular function notation is $f(x)$ which is read "$f$ of $x$".

### *Example:*

1) Evaluate: $w(x) = 3x + 1$, find $w(4)$. Substitute $x$ with 4: Then: $w(x) = 3x + 1 \rightarrow$

   $w(4) = 3(4) + 1 \rightarrow w(x) = 12 + 1 \rightarrow w(x) = 13$

2) Evaluate: $h(n) = n^2 - 10$, find $h(-2)$. Substitute $x$ with $-2$:

   Then: $h(n) = n^2 - 10 \rightarrow h(-2) = (-2)^2 - 10 \rightarrow h(-2) = 4 - 10 \rightarrow h(-2) = -6$

### *Evaluate each function.*

1) $f(x) = -x + 5$, find $f(4)$

2) $g(n) = 10n - 3$, find $g(6)$

3) $g(n) = 8n + 4$, find $g(1)$

4) $h(x) = 4x - 22$, find $h(2)$

5) $h(a) = -11a + 5$, find $h(2a)$

6) $k(a) = 7a + 3$, find $k(a - 2)$

7) $h(x) = 3x + 5$, find $h(6x)$

8) $h(n) = n^2 - 10$, find $h(5)$

9) $h(n) = -2n^2 - 6n$, find $h(2)$

10) $g(n) = 3n^2 + 2n$, find $g(2)$

11) $h(x) = x^2 + 1$, find $h(\frac{x}{4})$

12) $h(x) = x^3 + 8$, find $h(-2)$

# Adding and Subtracting Functions

**Step-by-step guide:**

✓ Just like we can add and subtract numbers, we can add and subtract functions. For example, if we had functions $f$ and $g$, we could create two new functions:

✓ $f + g$ and $f - g$.

*Example:*

1) $f(x) = 2x + 4$, $g(x) = x + 3$, **Find:** $(f - g)(1)$

$(f - g)(x) = f(x) - g(x)$, then: $(f - g)(x) = 2x + 4 - (x + 3) = 2x + 4 - x - 3 = x + 1$

Substitute $x$ with 1: $(f - g)(1) = 1 + 1 = 2$

2) $g(a) = 2a - 1$, $f(a) = -a - 4$, **Find:** $(g + f)(-1)$

$(g + f)(a) = g(a) + f(a)$, Then: $(g + f)(a) = 2a - 1 - a - 4 = a - 5$

Substitute $a$ with $-1$: $(g + f)(a) = a - 5 = -1 - 5 = -6$

✍ *Perform the indicated operation.*

1) $g(x) = 2x - 5$

  $h(x) = 4x + 5$

  Find: $g(3) - h(3)$

2) $h(3) = 3x + 3$

  $g(x) = -4x + 1$

  Find: $(h + g)(10)$

3) $f(x) = 4x - 3$

  $g(x) = x^3 + 2x$

  Find: $(f - g)(4)$

4) $h(n) = 4n + 5$

  $g(n) = 3n + 4$

  Find: $(h - g)(n)$

5) $g(x) = -x^2 - 1 - 2x$

  $f(x) = 5 + x$

  Find: $(g - f)(x)$

6) $g(t) = 2t + 5$

  $f(t) = -t^2 + 5$

  Find: $(g + f)(t)$

## Multiplying and Dividing Functions

**Step-by-step guide:**

- ✓ Just like we can multiply and divide numbers, we can multiply and divide functions. For example, if we had functions $f$ and $g$, we could create two new functions: $f \times g$, and $\frac{f}{g}$.

*Example:*

1) $g(x) = -x - 2, f(x) = 2x + 1$, Find: $(g.f)(2)$

$(g.f)(x) = g(x).f(x) = (-x - 2)(2x + 1) = -2x^2 - x - 4x - 2 = -2x^2 - 5x - 2$

Substitute $x$ with 2:

$(g.f)(x) = -2x^2 - 5x - 2 = -2(2)^2 - 5(2) - 2 = -8 - 10 - 2 = -20$

2) $f(x) = x + 4, h(x) = 5x - 2$, Find: $\left(\frac{f}{h}\right)(-1)$

$\left(\frac{f}{h}\right)(x) = \frac{f(x)}{h(x)} = \frac{x+4}{5x-2}$

Substitute $x$ with $-1$: $\left(\frac{f}{h}\right)(x) = \frac{x+4}{5x-2} = \frac{(-1)+4}{5(-1)-2} = \frac{3}{-7} = -\frac{3}{7}$

🖎 *Perform the indicated operation.*

1) $f(x) = 2a^2$

$g(x) = -5 + 3a$

Find $(\frac{f}{h})(2)$

2) $g(a) = 3a + 2$

$f(a) = 2a - 4$

Find $(\frac{g}{f})(3)$

3) $g(t) = t^2 + 3$

$h(t) = 4t - 3$

Find $(g.h)(-1)$

4) $g(n) = n^2 + 4 + 2n$

$h(n) = -3n + 2$

Find $(g.h)(1)$

5) $f(x) = 2x^3 - 5x^2$

$g(x) = 2x - 1$

Find $(f.g)(x)$

6) $f(x) = 3x - 1$

$g(x) = x^2 - x$

Find $(\frac{f}{g})(x)$

# Composition of Functions

**Step-by-step guide:**

- ✓ The term "composition of functions" (or "composite function") refers to the combining together of two or more functions in a manner where the output from one function becomes the input for the next function.
- ✓ The notation used for composition is: $(f \circ g)(x) = f(g(x))$

**Example:**

**1) Using** $f(x) = x + 2$ and $g(x) = 4x$, find: $f(g(1))$

$(f \circ g)(x) = f(g(x))$

Then: $(f \circ g)(x) = f(g(x)) = f(4x) = 4x + 2$

Substitute $x$ with 1: $(f \circ g)(1) = 4 + 2 = 6$

**2) Using** $f(x) = 5x + 4$ and $g(x) = x - 3$, find: $g(f(3))$
$(f \circ g)(x) = f(g(x))$

Then: $(g \circ f)(x) = g(f(x)) = g(5x + 4)$ *now substitute $x$ in $g(x)$ by $5x + 4$. Then:*
$g(5x + 4) = (5x + 4) - 3 = 5x + 4 - 3 = 5x + 1$

Substitute $x$ with 3: $(g \circ f)(x) = g(f(x)) = 5x + 1 = 5(3) + 1 = 15 = 1 = 16$

✍ **Using** $f(x) = 6x + 2$ **and** $g(x) = x - 3$, **find:**

1) $f(g(7))$                                   3) $g(f(3))$

2) $f(f(2))$                                   4) $g(g(x))$

✍ **Using** $f(x) = 7x + 4$ **and** $g(x) = 2x - 4$, **find:**

5) $f(g(3))$                                   7) $g(f(4))$

6) $f(f(3))$                                   8) $g(g(5))$

# Answers – Day 28

## Function Notation

1) 1

2) 57

3) 12

4) $-8$

5) $-22a + 5$

6) $7a - 11$

7) $18x + 5$

8) 0

9) $-20$

10) 16

11) $1 + \frac{1}{16}x^2$

12) 15

## Adding and Subtracting Functions

1) $-16$

2) $-6$

3) $-59$

4) $n + 1$

5) $-x^2 - 3x - 6$

6) $-t^2 + 2t + 10$

## Multiplying and Dividing Functions

1) $-\frac{2}{8} = -\frac{1}{4}$

2) $\frac{11}{2}$

3) $-28$

4) $-7$

5) $4x^4 - 12x^3 + 5x^2$

6) $\frac{3x-1}{x^2-x}$

## Composition of functions

1) 14

2) 86

3) 15

4) $x - 10$

5) 18

6) 179

7) 60

8) 8

# Day 29: Time to Test

- You'll need a pencil, a calculator, and a timer to take the test.

- It's okay to guess. You won't lose any points if you're wrong. So be sure to answer every question.

- After you've finished the test, review the answer key to see where you went wrong.

- **Calculators are only permitted for the first section of the TASC Test.**

- The TASC Mathematics test contains a formula sheet, which displays formulas relating to geometric measurement and certain algebra concepts. Formulas are provided to test-takers so that they may focus on application, rather than the memorization, of formulas.

- For each multiple-choice question, there are four possible answers. Choose which one is best. For grids in questions, write your answer in the answer boxes at the top of the grid. Then, as shown below fill in a bubble under each box in which you wrote your answer.

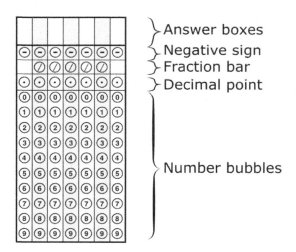

## Good Luck!

# TASC Mathematics Practice Test

# 2021

## Two Parts

**Total number of questions:** 52

**Part 1 (Calculator):** 40 questions

**Part 2 (Calculator):** 12 questions

**Total time for two parts:** 105 Minutes

# TASC Practice Tests Answer Sheet

**Remove (or photocopy) these answer sheets and use them to complete the practice tests.**

## TASC Practice Test – Section 1 Answer Sheet

| | | | | |
|---|---|---|---|---|
| 1 Ⓐ Ⓑ Ⓒ Ⓓ | 9 Ⓐ Ⓑ Ⓒ Ⓓ | 17 Ⓐ Ⓑ Ⓒ Ⓓ | 25 Ⓐ Ⓑ Ⓒ Ⓓ | 33 Ⓐ Ⓑ Ⓒ Ⓓ |
| 2 Ⓐ Ⓑ Ⓒ Ⓓ | 10 Ⓐ Ⓑ Ⓒ Ⓓ | 18 Ⓐ Ⓑ Ⓒ Ⓓ | 26 Ⓐ Ⓑ Ⓒ Ⓓ | 34 Ⓐ Ⓑ Ⓒ Ⓓ |
| 3 Ⓐ Ⓑ Ⓒ Ⓓ | 11 Ⓐ Ⓑ Ⓒ Ⓓ | 19 Ⓐ Ⓑ Ⓒ Ⓓ | 27 Ⓐ Ⓑ Ⓒ Ⓓ | 35 Ⓐ Ⓑ Ⓒ Ⓓ |
| 4 Ⓐ Ⓑ Ⓒ Ⓓ | 12 Ⓐ Ⓑ Ⓒ Ⓓ | 20 Ⓐ Ⓑ Ⓒ Ⓓ | 28 Ⓐ Ⓑ Ⓒ Ⓓ | 36 Ⓐ Ⓑ Ⓒ Ⓓ |
| 5 Ⓐ Ⓑ Ⓒ Ⓓ | 13 Ⓐ Ⓑ Ⓒ Ⓓ | 21 Ⓐ Ⓑ Ⓒ Ⓓ | 29 Ⓐ Ⓑ Ⓒ Ⓓ | 37 Ⓐ Ⓑ Ⓒ Ⓓ |
| 6 Ⓐ Ⓑ Ⓒ Ⓓ | 14 Ⓐ Ⓑ Ⓒ Ⓓ | 22 Ⓐ Ⓑ Ⓒ Ⓓ | 30 Ⓐ Ⓑ Ⓒ Ⓓ | 38 Ⓐ Ⓑ Ⓒ Ⓓ |
| 7 Ⓐ Ⓑ Ⓒ Ⓓ | 15 Ⓐ Ⓑ Ⓒ Ⓓ | 23 Ⓐ Ⓑ Ⓒ Ⓓ | 31 Ⓐ Ⓑ Ⓒ Ⓓ | 39 Ⓐ Ⓑ Ⓒ Ⓓ |
| 8 Ⓐ Ⓑ Ⓒ Ⓓ | 16 Ⓐ Ⓑ Ⓒ Ⓓ | 24 Ⓐ Ⓑ Ⓒ Ⓓ | 32 Ⓐ Ⓑ Ⓒ Ⓓ | 40 Ⓐ Ⓑ Ⓒ Ⓓ |

## TASC Practice Test: Section 2: Grid-ins Questions

41    42    43    44

**45**

**46**

**47**

**48**

**49**

**50**

**51**

**52**

# TASC Mathematics

# Practice Test

## Part 1 (Calculator)

**Total number of questions:** 40

**Total time for Part 1 (Calculator):** 55 Minutes

## You may use a calculator on this part.

# Mathematics Reference Sheet

**Cylinder:** $v = \pi r^2 h$

**Pyramid:** $v = \frac{1}{3} bh$

**cone:** $v = \frac{1}{3} \pi r^2 h$

**Sphere:** $\frac{4}{3} \pi r^3$

## coordinate Geometry

**Midpoint of the segment AB:**

$M \left( \dfrac{x_1 + x_2}{2}, \dfrac{y_1 + y_2}{2} \right)$

**Distance from A to B:**

$d = \sqrt{(x_1 - x_2)^2 + (y_1 - y_2)^2}$

**Slope of a line:**

$m = \dfrac{y_2 - y_1}{x_2 - x_1} = \dfrac{rise}{run}$

## Special Factoring

$a^2 - b^2 = (a + b)(a - b)$

$a^2 + 2ab + b^2 = (a + b)(a + b)$

$a^2 - 2ab + b^2 = (a - b)(a - b)$

$a^3 + b^3 = (a + b)(a^2 - ab + b^2)$

$a^3 - b^3 = (a - b)(a^2 + ab + b^2)$

## Quadratic Formula

for $ax^2 + bx + c = 0$

$x = \dfrac{-b \pm \sqrt{b^2 - 4ac}}{2a}$

## Interest

**Simple Interest:**

$I = prt$

**Interest Formula (compounded $n$ times per year):**

$A = p \left( 1 + \dfrac{r}{n} \right)^{nt}$

A = Amount after $t$ years.

p = principal

r = annual interest rate

t = time in years

I = Interest

## Trigonometric Identities

Pythagorean Theorem: $a^2 + b^2 = c^2$

$\sin \theta = \dfrac{opp}{hyp}$

$\cos \theta = \dfrac{adj}{hyp}$

$\tan \theta = \dfrac{opp}{adj}$

$\sin^2 \theta + \cos^2 \theta = 1$

$Density = \dfrac{Mass}{Volume}$

| Central Angle | Inscribed Angle | Intersecting Chords Theorem |
|---|---|---|
|  |  | 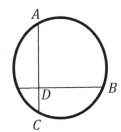 |
| $m\angle AOB = m\widehat{AB}$ | $m\angle ABC = \frac{1}{2}m\widehat{AC}$ | $A \cdot B = C \cdot D$ |

**Probability**

Permutations: $_nP_r = \dfrac{n!}{(n-r)!}$

Combinations: $_nC_r = \dfrac{n!}{(n-r)!\,r!}$

Multiplication rule (independent events): P(A and B) = P(A)·P(B)

Multiplication rule (general): P(A and B) = P(A)·P(B|A)

Addition rule: P(A or B) = P(A) + P(B) − P(A and B)

Conditional Probability: P(B|A) = $\dfrac{P(A \text{ and } B)}{P(A)}$

Arithmetic Sequence: $a_n = a_1 + (n-1)d$ where $a_n$ is the $n$th term, $a_1$ is the first term, and $d$ is the common difference.

Geometric Sequence: $a_n = a_1 r^{(n-1)}$ where $a_n$ is the $n$th term, $a_1$ is the first term, and $r$ is the common ratio.

1) When a number is subtracted from 28 and the difference is divided by that number, the result is 3. What is the value of the number?

A. 2

B. 4

C. 7

D. 12

2) An angle is equal to one fifth of its supplement. What is the measure of that angle?

A. 18

B. 24

C. 30

D. 45

3) John traveled 150 $km$ in 6 hours and Alice traveled 180 $km$ in 4 hours. What is the ratio of the average speed of John to average speed of Alice?

A. 3 : 2

B. 2 : 3

C. 5 : 9

D. 5 : 6

4) A taxi driver earns \$8 per 1 —hour work. If he works 10 hours a day and in 1 hour he uses 2 —liters petrol with price \$1 for 1 —liter. How much money does he earn in one day?

A. \$80

B. \$88

C. \$60

D. \$60

5) Find the average of the following numbers: $15, 13, 7, 21, 19$

A. 17

B. 16.5

C. 15

D. 11

6) The price of a sofa is decreased by 20% to $476. What was its original price?

A. $480

B. $520

C. $595

D. $600

7) Right triangle $ABC$ has two legs of lengths $5\ cm\ (AB)$ and $12\ cm\ (AC)$. What is the length of the third side $(BC)$?

A. $6\ cm$

B. $8\ cm$

C. $10\ cm$

D. $13\ cm$

8) If 45% of a class are girls, and 25% of girls play tennis, what percent of the class play tennis?

A. 11%

B. 15%

C. 20%

D. 40%

9)    The area of a circle is less than $49\pi$. Which of the following can be the circumference of the circle?

A. $12\pi$

B. $14\pi$

C. $24\pi$

D. $32\pi$

10)    Which of the following values for $x$ and $y$ satisfy the following system of equations?

$$\begin{cases} x + 4y = 10 \\ 5x + 10y = 20 \end{cases}$$

A.    $x = 3, y = 2$

B.    $x = 2, y - 3$

C.    $x = -2, y = 3$

D.    $x = 3, y = -2$

11)    If 60% of A is 30% of B, then B is what percent of A?

A. 2%

B. 20%

C. 200%

D. 300%

12)    The price of a car was $20,000 in 2014, $16,000 in 2015 and $12,800 in 2016. What is the rate of depreciation of the price of car per year?

A.15%

B. 20%

C.25%

D. 30%

13) The width of a box is one third of its length. The height of the box is one third of its width. If the length of the box is $54\ cm$, what is the volume of the box?

A. $81\ cm^3$

B. $162\ cm^3$

C. $243\ cm^3$

D. $5,832\ cm^3$

14) How many possible outfit combinations come from six shirts, four slacks, and five ties?

A.  15

B.  18

C.  30

D.  120

15) A bank is offering 3.5% simple interest on a savings account. If you deposit $8,000, how much interest will you earn in five years?

A. $360

B. $720

C. $1,400

D. $3,600

16) If $x$ is directly proportional to the square of $y$, and $y = 2$ when $x = 12$, then when $x = 75$ $y = ?$

A. $\dfrac{1}{5}$

B. 1

C. 5

D. 12

17)     Jack earns $616 for his first 44 hours of work in a week and is then paid 1.5 times his regular hourly rate for any additional hours. This week, Jack needs $826 to pay his rent, bills and other expenses. How many hours must he work to make enough money in this week?

A. 40

B. 53

C. 48

D. 54

18)     If the area of trapezoid is 126 $cm$, what is the perimeter of the trapezoid?

A. 12 $cm$

B. 32 $cm$

C. 46 $cm$

D. 55 $cm$

19)     In five successive hours, a car traveled 40 $km$, 45 $km$, 50 $km$, 35 $km$ and 55 $km$. In the next five hours, it traveled with an average speed of 65 $km$ per hour. Find the total distance the car traveled in 10 hours.

A. 425 $km$

B. 450 $km$

C. 475 $km$

D. 560 $km$

20)     How long does a 420– miles trip take moving at 50 miles per hour ($mph$)?

A. 4 hours

B. 6 hours and 24 minutes

C. 8 hours and 24 minutes

D. 8 hours and 30 minutes

21)    In the $xy$-plane, the point $(4, 3)$ and $(3, 2)$ are on line $A$. Which of the following points could also be on line $A$? (Select one or more answer choices)

A. $(-1, 2)$

B. $(5, 7)$

C. $(3, 4)$

D. $(-1, -2)$

22)    Two third of 15 is equal to $\frac{2}{5}$ of what number?

A. 12

B. 20

C. 25

D. 60

23)    The marked price of a computer is $D$ dollar. Its price decreased by 20% in January and later increased by 10% in February. What is the final price of the computer in $D$ dollar?

A. $0.80\ D$

B. $0.88\ D$

C. $0.90\ D$

D. $1.20\ D$

24)    In the rectangle below if $y > 5\ cm$ and the area of rectangle is $50\ cm^2$ and the perimeter of the rectangle is $30\ cm$, what is the value of $x$ and $y$ respectively?

A. $4, 11$

B. $5, 11$

C. $5, 10$

D. $4, 10$

25) What is the length of AB in the following figure if AE = 4, CD = 6 and AC = 12?

A. 3.8

C. 4.8

B. 7.2

D. 24

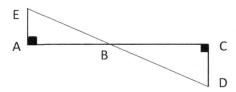

26) If a gas tank can hold 25 gallons, how many gallons does it contain when it is $\frac{2}{5}$ full?

A. 50

C. 125

B. 62.5

D. 10

27) What is the area of the shaded region?

A. 31 $ft$

C. 40 $ft$

B. 64 $ft$

D. 80 $ft$

28) The ratio of boys and girls in a class is 4: 7. If there are 44 students in the class, how many more boys should be enrolled to make the ratio 1: 1?

A. 8

B. 10

C. 12

D. 16

29) In the following right triangle, if the sides $AB$ and $AC$ become twice longer, what will be the ratio of the perimeter of the triangle to its area?

A. $\frac{1}{2}$

B. 2

C. $\frac{1}{3}$

D. 3

30) Which of the following is the same as: 0.000 000 000 000 042 121?

A. $4.2121 \times 10^{14}$

B. $4.2121 \times 10^{-14}$

C. $42,121 \times 10^{-10}$

D. $42.121 \times 10^{-13}$

31) A bag contains 18 balls: two green, five black, eight blue, a brown, a red and one white. If 17 balls are removed from the bag at random, what is the probability that a brown ball has been removed?

A. $\dfrac{1}{9}$

B. $\dfrac{1}{6}$

C. $\dfrac{16}{17}$

D. $\dfrac{17}{18}$

32) The average of five consecutive numbers is 40. What is the smallest number?

A. 38

B. 36

C. 34

D. 12

33) What is the area of the shaded region if the diameter of the bigger circle is 12 inches and the diameter of the smaller circle is 8 inches?

A. $16\pi$

B. $20\pi$

C. $36\pi$

D. $80\pi$

34) A rope weighs 600 grams per meter of length. What is the weight in kilograms of 12.2 meters of this rope? (1 kilograms $=$ 1000 grams)

A. 0.0732

B. 0.732

C. 7.32

D. 73.20

35) A chemical solution contains 6% alcohol. If there is 24 $ml$ of alcohol, what is the volume of the solution?

A. 240 $ml$

B. 400 $ml$

C. 600 $ml$

D. 1200 $ml$

36) The average weight of 18 girls in a class is $60\ kg$ and the average weight of 32 boys in the same class is $62\ kg$. What is the average weight of all the 50 students in that class?

A. 60

B. 61.28

C. 61.68

D. 62.90

37) The price of a laptop is decreased by 25% to $360. What is its original price?

A. 320

B. 380

C. 480

D. 550

38) What is the median of these numbers? $1, 12, 13, 8, 15, 18, 5$

A. 8

B. 12

C. 13

D. 15

39) A student gets an 85% on a test with 40 questions. How many answers did the student solve correctly?

A. 25

B. 28

C. 34

D. 36

40) The capacity of a red box is 20% bigger than the capacity of a blue box. If the red box can hold 30 equal sized books, how many of the same books can the blue box hold?

A. 9

B. 15

C. 21

D. 25

IF YOU FINISH BEFORE TIME IS CALLED, YOU MAY CHECK YOUR WORK ON THIS SECTION ONLY. DO NOT TURN TO OTHER SECTION IN THE TEST.    STOP

# TASC Mathematics

# Practice Test

## Part 2 (Non-Calculator)

**Total number of questions:** 12

**Total time for Part 1 (Calculator):** 50 Minutes

# You may NOT use a calculator on this part.

41) If $3x - 5 = 8.5$, What is the value of $6x + 3$ ?

42) What is the area of an isosceles right triangle that has one leg that measures 12?

43) The perimeter of the trapezoid below is 54. What is its area?

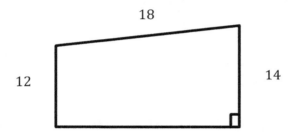

44) From last year, the price of gasoline has increased from $1.25 per gallon to $1.75 per gallon. The new price is what percent of the original price?

45) $-18 + 6 \times (-5) - [4 + 22 \times (-4)] \div 2 + 9 = ?$

46) A ladder leans against a wall forming a 60° angle between the ground and the ladder. If the bottom of the ladder is 45 feet away from the wall, how many feet is the ladder?

47) The volume of cube A is $\frac{1}{3}$ of its surface area. What is the length of an edge of cube A?

48) What is the value of $f(4)$ for the following function $f$?

$$f(x) = x^2 - 3x$$

49) If $\frac{x-3}{5} = N$ and $N = 5$, what is the value of $x$?

50) If the ratio of $5a$ to $2b$ is $\frac{1}{8}$, what is the ratio of $a$ to $b$?

51) A construction company is building a wall. The company can build $30\ cm$ of the wall per minute. After 40 minutes $\frac{3}{4}$ of the wall is completed. How many meters is the wall?

52) The average of $13, 15, 20$ and $x$ is $18$. What is the value of $x$?

**IF YOU FINISH BEFORE TIME IS CALLED, YOU MAY CHECK YOUR WORK ON THIS SECTION ONLY. DO NOT TURN TO OTHER SECTION IN THE TEST.**

**STOP**

# TASC Mathematics Practice Test Answers and Explanations

Now, it's time to review your results to see where you went wrong and what areas you need to improve!

| TASC Practice Test Answer Key | | | | | | | |
|---|---|---|---|---|---|---|---|
| 1 | C | 16 | C | 31 | D | 41 | 30 |
| 2 | C | 17 | C | 32 | A | 42 | 18 |
| 3 | C | 18 | C | 33 | B | 43 | 130 |
| 4 | C | 19 | C | 34 | C | 44 | 140 |
| 5 | C | 20 | C | 35 | B | 45 | 3 |
| 6 | C | 21 | D | 36 | B | 46 | 90 |
| 7 | D | 22 | C | 37 | C | 47 | 2 |
| 8 | A | 23 | B | 38 | B | 48 | 4 |
| 9 | A | 24 | C | 39 | D | 49 | 28 |
| 10 | C | 25 | C | 40 | D | 50 | 0.05 |
| 11 | C | 26 | D | | | 51 | 16 |
| 12 | B | 27 | C | | | 52 | 24 |
| 13 | D | 28 | C | | | | |
| 14 | D | 29 | B | | | | |
| 15 | C | 30 | B | | | | |

# TASC Mathematics Practice Test

# Answers and Explanations

### 1) Choice C is correct

Let $x$ be the number. Write the equation and solve for $x$. $(28 - x) \div x = 3$. Multiply both sides by $x$. $(28 - x) = 3x$, then add $x$ both sides. $28 = 4x$, now divide both sides by 4.

$x = 7$

### 2) Choice C is correct

The sum of supplement angles is 180. Let $x$ be that angle. Therefore, $x + 5x = 180$, $6x = 180$, divide both sides by 6: $x = 30$

### 3) Choice C is correct

The average speed of john is: $150 \div 6 = 25 \ km$, The average speed of Alice is: $180 \div 4 = 45 \ km$. Write the ratio and simplify. $25 : 45 \Rightarrow 5 : 9$

### 4) Choice C is correct

$\$8 \times 10 = \$80$,      Petrol use:     $10 \times 2 = 20$ liters

Petrol cost:    $20 \times \$1 = \$20$, Money earned:     $\$80 - \$20 = \$60$

### 5) Choice C is correct

$$average = \frac{sum \ of \ terms}{number \ of \ terms} = \frac{15 + 13 + 7 + 21 + 19}{5} = \frac{75}{5} = 15$$

### 6) Choice C is correct

Let $x$ be the original price. If the price of the sofa is decreased by 20% to \$476, then: $80\% \ of \ x = 476 \Rightarrow 0.80x = 476 \Rightarrow x = 476 \div 0.80 = 595$

### 7) Choice D is correct

Use Pythagorean Theorem: $a^2 + b^2 = c^2$

$$5^2 + 12^2 = c^2 \Rightarrow 25 + 144 = c^2 \Rightarrow 169 = c^2 \Rightarrow c = 13$$

**8) Choice A is correct**

The percent of girls playing tennis is: $45\% \times 25\% = 0.45 \times 0.25 = 0.11 = 11\%$

**9) Choice A is correct**

Area of the circle is less than $14\,\pi$. Use the formula of areas of circles.

$$Area = \pi r^2 \Rightarrow 49\,\pi > \pi r^2 \Rightarrow 49 > r^2 \Rightarrow r < 7$$

Radius of the circle is less than 7. Let's put 7 for the radius. Now, use the circumference formula:

Circumference $= 2\pi r = 2\pi\,(7) = 14\,\pi$

Since the radius of the circle is less than 7. Then, the circumference of the circle must be less than $14\,\pi$. Only choice A is less than $14\,\pi$.

**10) Choice C is correct**

$\begin{cases} x + 4y = 10 \\ 5x + 10y = 20 \end{cases} \rightarrow$    Multiply the top equation by $-5$ then,

$\begin{cases} -5x - 20y = -50 \\ 5x + 10y = 20 \end{cases} \rightarrow$      Add two equations

$-10y = -30 \rightarrow y = 3$ , plug in the value of $y$ into the first equation

$x + 4y = 10 \rightarrow x + 4(3) = 10 \rightarrow x + 12 = 10$

Subtract 12 from both sides of the equation. Then: $x + 12 = 10 \rightarrow x = -2$

**11) Choice C is correct**

Write the equation and solve for $B$: $0.60\,A = 0.30\,B$, divide both sides by $0.30$, then: $\frac{0.60}{0.30}\,A = B$, therefore: $B = 2A$, and $B$ is 2 times of $A$ or it's 200% of $A$.

**12) Choice B is correct**

Use this formula: Percent of Change $\dfrac{New\ Value - Old\ Value}{Old\ Value} \times 100\%$

$\dfrac{16{,}000 - 20{,}000}{20{,}000} \times 100\% = -20\%$ and $\dfrac{12{,}800 - 16{,}000}{16{,}000} \times 100\% = -20\%$

**13) Choice D is correct**

If the length of the box is 54, then the width of the box is one third of it, 18, and the height of the box is 6 (one third of the width). The volume of the box is:

$$V = lwh = (54)(18)(6) = 5,832$$

**14) Choice D is correct**

To find the number of possible outfit combinations, multiply number of options for each factor:

$$6 \times 4 \times 5 = 120$$

**15) Choice C is correct**

Use simple interest formula: $I = prt$ ($I = interest, p = principal, r = rate, t = time$)

$$I = (8,000)(0.035)(5) = 1,400$$

**16) Choice C is correct**

$x$ is directly proportional to the square of $y$. Then: $x = cy^2 \rightarrow 12 = c(2)^2 \rightarrow 12 = 4c \rightarrow c = \frac{12}{4} = 3$. The relationship between $x$ and $y$ is: $x = 3y^2$, $x = 75$

$$75 = 3y^2 \rightarrow y^2 = \frac{75}{3} = 25 \rightarrow y = 5$$

**17) Choice D is correct**

The amount of money that jack earns for one hour: $\frac{\$616}{44} = \$14$

Number of additional hours that he works to make enough money is: $\frac{\$826 - \$616}{1.5 \times \$14} = 10$

Number of total hours is: $44 + 10 = 54$

**18) Choice C is correct**

The area of the trapezoid is: $Area = \frac{1}{2}h(b_1 + b_2) = \frac{1}{2}(x)(13 + 8) = 126 \rightarrow$

$10.5x = 126 \rightarrow x = 12.$    $y = \sqrt{5^2 + 12^2} = \sqrt{25 + 144} = \sqrt{169} = 13$

The perimeter of the trapezoid is:    $12 + 13 + 8 + 13 = 46$

**19) Choice C is correct**

Add the first 5 numbers. $40 + 45 + 50 + 35 + 55 = 225$

To find the distance traveled in the next 5 hours, multiply the average by number of hours.

$Distance = Average \times Rate = 50 \times 5 = 250$

Add both numbers. $250 + 225 = 475$

**20) Choice C is correct**

Use distance formula: $Distance = Rate \times time \Rightarrow 420 = 50 \times T$, divide both sides by 50.
$420 \div 50 = T \Rightarrow T = 8.4$ hours

Change hours to minutes for the decimal part. $0.4\ hours = 0.4 \times 60 = 24\ minutes$

**21) Choice D is correct**

The equation of a line is in the form of $y = mx + b$, where $m$ is the slope of the line and $b$ is the $y - intercept$ of the line. Two points $(4, 3)$ and $(3, 2)$ are on line A. Therefore, the slope of the line A is: $slope\ of\ line\ A = \frac{y_2 - y_1}{x_2 - x_1} = \frac{2-3}{3-4} = \frac{-1}{-1} = 1$

The slope of line A is 1. Thus, the formula of the line A is: $y = mx + b = x + b$, choose a point and plug in the values of $x$ and $y$ in the equation to solve for $b$. Let's choose point $(4, 3)$. Then:
$y = x + b \rightarrow 3 = 4 + b \rightarrow b = 3 - 4 = -1$

The equation of line A is: $y = x - 1$

Now, let's review the choices provided:

A. $(-1, 2)$          $y = x - 1 \rightarrow 2 = -1 - 1 = -2$     This is not true.

B. $(5, 7)$          $y = x - 1 \rightarrow 7 = 5 - 1 = 4$     This is not true.

C. $(3, 4)$          $y = x - 1 \rightarrow 4 = 3 - 1 = 2$     This is not true.

D. $(-1, -2)$          $y = x - 1 \rightarrow -2 = -1 - 1 = -2$     This is true!

### 22) Choice C is correct

Let $x$ be the number. Write the equation and solve for $x$. $\frac{2}{3} \times 15 = \frac{2}{5} \cdot x \Rightarrow \frac{2 \times 15}{3} = \frac{2x}{5}$, use

cross multiplication to solve for $x$. $5 \times 30 = 2x \times 3 \Rightarrow 150 = 6x \Rightarrow x = 25$

### 23) Choice B is correct

To find the discount, multiply the number by $(100\% - rate\ of\ discount)$.

Therefore, for the first discount we get: $(D)(100\% - 20\%) = (D)\ (0.80) = 0.80\ D$

For increase of $10\%$: $(0.80\ D)(100\% + 10\%) = (0.80\ D)(1.10) = 0.88\ D = 88\%\ of\ D$

### 24) Choice C is correct

The perimeter of the rectangle is: $2x + 2y = 30 \rightarrow x + y = 15 \rightarrow x = 15 - y$

The area of the rectangle is: $x \times y = 50 \rightarrow (15 - y)(y) = 50 \rightarrow y^2 - 15y + 50 = 0$

Solve the quadratic equation by factoring method. $(y - 5)(y - 10) = 0 \rightarrow y = 5$

(Unacceptable, because $y$ must be greater than 5) or $y = 10$

If $y = 10 \rightarrow x \times y = 50 \rightarrow x \times 10 = 50 \rightarrow x = 5$

### 25) Choice C is correct

Two triangles $\Delta BAE$ and $\Delta BCD$ are similar. Then: $\frac{AE}{CD} = \frac{AB}{BC} \rightarrow \frac{4}{6} = \frac{x}{12} \rightarrow 48 - 4x = 6x \rightarrow$

$$10x = 48 \rightarrow x = 4.8$$

### 26) Choice D is correct

$\frac{2}{5} \times 25 = \frac{50}{5} = 10$

### 27) Choice C is correct

Use the area of rectangle formula (A = length × width). Let $A_1$ be the area of bigger rectangle and $A_2$ be the area of smaller rectangle. To find area of the shaded region subtract smaller rectangle from bigger rectangle. $A_1 - A_2 = (10ft \times 8ft) - (5ft \times 8ft) \Rightarrow A_1 - A_2 = 40ft$

**28) Choice C is correct**

The ratio of boy to girls is $4:7$. Therefore, there are 4 boys out of 11 students. To find the answer, first divide the total number of students by 11, then multiply the result by 4.

$44 \div 11 = 4 \Rightarrow 4 \times 4 = 16$. There are 16 boys and 28 $(44 - 16)$ girls. So, 12 more boys should be enrolled to make the ratio $1:1$.

**29) Choice A is correct**

$AB = 12$       And     $AC = 5$. $BC = \sqrt{12^2 + 5^2} = \sqrt{144 + 25} = \sqrt{169} = 13$

Perimeter $= 5 + 12 + 13 = 30$.       Area $= \frac{5 \times 12}{2} = 5 \times 6 = 30$

In this case, the ratio of the perimeter of the triangle to its area is: $\frac{30}{30} = 1$

If the sides AB and AC become twice longer, then: $AB = 24$       And     $AC = 10$

$BC = \sqrt{24^2 + 10^2} = \sqrt{576 + 100} = \sqrt{676} = 26$. Perimeter $= 26 + 24 + 10 = 60$

Area $= \frac{10 \times 24}{2} = 10 \times 12 = 120$

In this case the ratio of the perimeter of the triangle to its area is: $\frac{60}{120} = \frac{1}{2}$

**30) Choice B is correct**

In scientific notation all numbers are written in the form of: $m \times 10^n$, where $m$ is between 1 and 10. To find an equivalent value of $0.000\,000\,000\,000\,042\,121$, move the decimal point to the right so that you have a number that is between 1 and 10.  Then: $4.2121$
Now, determine how many places the decimal moved in step 1, then put it as the power of 10. We moved the decimal point 14 places. Then: $10^{-14} \rightarrow$ When the decimal moved to the right, the exponent is negative. Then: $0.000\,000\,000\,000\,042\,121 = 4.2121 \times 10^{-14}$

**31) Choice D is correct**

If 17 balls are removed from the bag at random, there will be one ball in the bag. The probability of choosing a brown ball is 1 out of 18. Therefore, the probability of not choosing a brown ball is 17 out of 18 and the probability of having not a brown ball after removing 17 balls is the same.

**32) Choice A is correct**

Let $x$ be the smallest number. Then, these are the numbers: $x, x + 1, x + 2, x + 3, x + 4$

$$average = \frac{sum\ of\ terms}{number\ of\ terms} \Rightarrow 40 = \frac{x + (x + 1) + (x + 2) + (x + 3) + (x + 4)}{5} \Rightarrow 40$$

$$= \frac{5x + 10}{5} \Rightarrow$$

$$200 = 5x + 10 \Rightarrow 190 = 5x \Rightarrow x = 38$$

**33) Choice B is correct.**

To find the area of the shaded region subtract smaller circle from bigger circle.

$$S_{bigger} - S_{smaller} = \pi\ (r_{bigger})^2 - \pi\ (r_{smaller})^2 \Rightarrow S_{bigger} - S_{smaller} = \pi\ (6)^2 - \pi\ (4)^2$$

$$\Rightarrow 36\pi - 16\pi = 20\pi$$

**34) Choice C is correct**

The weight of 12.2 meters of this rope is: $12.2 \times 600\ g = 7,320\ g$

$1\ kg = 1,000\ g$, therefore, $7,320\ g \div 1,000 = 7.32\ kg$

**35) Choice B is correct**

6% of the volume of the solution is alcohol. Let $x$ be the volume of the solution.

Then: $6\%\ of\ x = 24\ ml \Rightarrow 0.06\ x = 24 \Rightarrow x = 24 \div 0.06 = 400$

**36) Choice B is correct**

average $= \frac{sum\ of\ terms}{number\ of\ terms}$. The sum of the weight of all girls is: $18 \times 60 = 1,080\ kg$, The sum

of the weight of all boys is: $32 \times 62 = 1,984\ kg$, The sum of the weight of all students is:

$1,080 + 1,984 = 3,064\ kg$. average $= \frac{3,064}{50} = 61.28$

**37) Choice C is correct**

Let $x$ be the original price. If the price of a laptop is decreased by 25% to $360, then:

$$75\%\ of\ x = 360 \rightarrow 0.75x = 360 \rightarrow x = 360 \div 0.75 = 480$$

**38) Choice B is correct**

Write the numbers in order: $1, 5, 8, 12, 13, 15, 18$. Since we have 7 numbers (7 is odd), then the median is the number in the middle, which is 12.

**39) Choice D is correct**

85% of 40 is: $85\% \ of \ 40 = 0.85 \times 40 = 34$. So, the student solves 34 questions correctly.

**40) Choice D is correct**

The capacity of a red box is 20% bigger than the capacity of a blue box and it can hold 30 books. Therefore, we want to find a number that 20% bigger than that number is 30. Let $x$ be that number. Then: $1.20 \times x = 30$, Divide both sides of the equation by 1.2. Then: $x = \frac{30}{1.20} = 25$

**41) The answer is 30**

$3x - 5 = 8.5 \rightarrow 3x = 8.5 + 5 = 13.5 \rightarrow x = \frac{13.5}{3} = 4.5$ , Then; $6x + 3 = 6 \ (4.5) + 3 = 27 + 3 = 30$

**42) The answer is 18**

First draw an isosceles triangle. Remember that two sides of the triangle are equal.

Isosceles right triangle

Let put $a$ for the legs. Then:

$a = 12 \Rightarrow$ area of the triangle is $= \frac{1}{2} (12 \times 12) = \frac{144}{2} = 72$

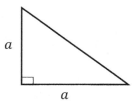

**43) The answer is 130**

The perimeter of the trapezoid is 54.

Therefore, the missing side (height) is $= 54 - 18 - 12 - 14 = 10$

Area of a trapezoid: $A = \frac{1}{2} \ h \ (b_1 + b_2) = \frac{1}{2} (10)(12 + 14) = 130$

**44) The answer is 140**

$x = \dfrac{175}{1.25} = 140$

**45) The answer is 3**

Use PEMDAS (order of operation):

$$-18 + 6 \times (-5) - [4 + 22 \times (-4)] \div 2 + 9 = -18 - 30 - [4 - 88] \div 2 + 9$$

$$= -48 - [-84] \div 2 + 9 = -48 + 84 \div 2 + 9 = -48 + 42 + 9 = 3$$

**46) The answer is 90**

The relationship among all sides of special right triangle

$30° - 60° - 90°$ is provided in this triangle:

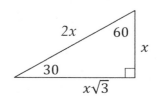

In this triangle, the opposite side of $30°$ angle is half of the hypotenuse.

Draw the shape of this question. The latter is the hypotenuse. Therefore, the latter is 90 feet.

**47) The answer is 2**

Let $x$ be the length of an edge of cube, then the volume of a cube is:     $V = x^3$

The surface area of cube is:   $SA = 6x^2$

The volume of cube A is $\frac{1}{3}$ of its surface area. Then: $x^3 = \frac{6x^2}{3} \rightarrow x^3 = 2x^2$, divide both side of the

equation by $x^2$. Then: $\frac{x^3}{x^2} = \frac{2x^2}{x^2} \rightarrow x = 2$

**48) The answer is 4**

The input value is 5. Then: $x = 4, f(x) = x^2 - 3x \rightarrow f(4) = 4^2 - 3(4) = 16 - 12 = 4$

**49) The answer is 28**

Since $N = 5$, substitute 5 for $N$ in the equation $\frac{x-3}{5} = N$, which gives $\frac{x-3}{5} = 5$. Multiplying both

sides of $\frac{x-3}{5} = 5$ by 5 gives $x - 3 = 25$ and then adding 3 to both sides of $x - 3 = 25$ then, $x = 28$.

**50) The answer is $\frac{1}{20}$ or $0.05$**

Write the ratio of $5a$ to $2b$. $\frac{5a}{2b} = \frac{1}{8}$

Use cross multiplication and then simplify. $5a \times 8 = 2b \times 1 \rightarrow 40a = 2b \rightarrow a = \frac{2b}{40} = \frac{b}{20}$

Now, find the ratio of $a$ to $b$. $\dfrac{a}{b} = \dfrac{\frac{b}{20}}{b} \rightarrow \dfrac{b}{20} \div b = \dfrac{b}{20} \times \dfrac{1}{b} = \dfrac{b}{20b} = \dfrac{1}{20} = 0.05$

### 51) The answer is 16

The rate of construction company $= \dfrac{30\ cm}{1\ min} = 30\ \dfrac{cm}{min}$

Height of the wall after 40 minutes $= \dfrac{30\ cm}{1\ min} \times 40\ min = 1{,}200\ cm$

Let $x$ be the height of wall, then $\dfrac{3}{4}x = 1{,}200\ cm \rightarrow x = \dfrac{4 \times 1{,}200}{3} \rightarrow x = 1{,}600\ cm = 16\ m$

### 52) The answer is 24

$$average = \dfrac{sum\ of\ terms}{number\ of\ terms} \Rightarrow 18 = \dfrac{13 + 15 + 20 + x}{4} \Rightarrow 72 = 48 + x \Rightarrow x = 24$$

# Day 30: A Realistic TASC Math Test

## Time to experience a REAL TASC Math Test

Take the following practice TASC Math Test to simulate the test day experience. After you've finished, score your test using the answer key.

## Before You Start

- Keep your practice test experience as realistic as possible.

- You'll need a pencil, calculator, and a timer to take the test.

- It's okay to guess. You won't lose any points if you're wrong.

- After you've finished the test, review the answer key to see where you went go.

- **Keep Strict Timing on the Test Section!**

## *Good Luck!*

*Mathematics is not only real, but it is the only reality. — Martin Gardner*

# TASC Mathematics

# Practice Test

# 2021

## Two Parts

**Total number of questions:** 52

**Part 1 (Calculator):** 40 questions

**Part 2 (Calculator):** 12 questions

**Total time for two parts:** 105 Minutes

# TASC Practice Tests Answer Sheet

**Remove (or photocopy) these answer sheets and use them to complete the practice tests.**

| TASC Practice Test – Section 1 Answer Sheet | | | | |
|---|---|---|---|---|
| 1 Ⓐ Ⓑ Ⓒ Ⓓ | 9 Ⓐ Ⓑ Ⓒ Ⓓ | 17 Ⓐ Ⓑ Ⓒ Ⓓ | 25 Ⓐ Ⓑ Ⓒ Ⓓ | 33 Ⓐ Ⓑ Ⓒ Ⓓ |
| 2 Ⓐ Ⓑ Ⓒ Ⓓ | 10 Ⓐ Ⓑ Ⓒ Ⓓ | 18 Ⓐ Ⓑ Ⓒ Ⓓ | 26 Ⓐ Ⓑ Ⓒ Ⓓ | 34 Ⓐ Ⓑ Ⓒ Ⓓ |
| 3 Ⓐ Ⓑ Ⓒ Ⓓ | 11 Ⓐ Ⓑ Ⓒ Ⓓ | 19 Ⓐ Ⓑ Ⓒ Ⓓ | 27 Ⓐ Ⓑ Ⓒ Ⓓ | 35 Ⓐ Ⓑ Ⓒ Ⓓ |
| 4 Ⓐ Ⓑ Ⓒ Ⓓ | 12 Ⓐ Ⓑ Ⓒ Ⓓ | 20 Ⓐ Ⓑ Ⓒ Ⓓ | 28 Ⓐ Ⓑ Ⓒ Ⓓ | 36 Ⓐ Ⓑ Ⓒ Ⓓ |
| 5 Ⓐ Ⓑ Ⓒ Ⓓ | 13 Ⓐ Ⓑ Ⓒ Ⓓ | 21 Ⓐ Ⓑ Ⓒ Ⓓ | 29 Ⓐ Ⓑ Ⓒ Ⓓ | 37 Ⓐ Ⓑ Ⓒ Ⓓ |
| 6 Ⓐ Ⓑ Ⓒ Ⓓ | 14 Ⓐ Ⓑ Ⓒ Ⓓ | 22 Ⓐ Ⓑ Ⓒ Ⓓ | 30 Ⓐ Ⓑ Ⓒ Ⓓ | 38 Ⓐ Ⓑ Ⓒ Ⓓ |
| 7 Ⓐ Ⓑ Ⓒ Ⓓ | 15 Ⓐ Ⓑ Ⓒ Ⓓ | 23 Ⓐ Ⓑ Ⓒ Ⓓ | 31 Ⓐ Ⓑ Ⓒ Ⓓ | 39 Ⓐ Ⓑ Ⓒ Ⓓ |
| 8 Ⓐ Ⓑ Ⓒ Ⓓ | 16 Ⓐ Ⓑ Ⓒ Ⓓ | 24 Ⓐ Ⓑ Ⓒ Ⓓ | 32 Ⓐ Ⓑ Ⓒ Ⓓ | 40 Ⓐ Ⓑ Ⓒ Ⓓ |

| TASC Practice Test: Section 2: Grid-ins Questions |
|---|

41    42    43    44

**45**

**46**

**47**

**48**

**49**

**50**

**51**

**52**

# TASC Mathematics

# Practice Test

## Part 1 (Calculator)

**Total number of questions:** 40

**Total time for Part 1 (Calculator):** 55 Minutes

## You may use a calculator on this part.

# Mathematics Reference Sheet

**Cylinder:** $v = \pi r^2 h$

**Pyramid:** $v = \frac{1}{3}bh$

**cone:** $v = \frac{1}{3}\pi r^2 h$

**Sphere:** $\frac{4}{3}\pi r^3$

## coordinate Geometry

**Midpoint of the segment AB:**

$$M\left(\frac{x_1 + x_2}{2}, \frac{y_1 + y_2}{2}\right)$$

**Distance from A to B:**

$$d = \sqrt{(x_1 - x_2)^2 + (y_1 - y_2)^2}$$

**Slope of a line:**

$$m = \frac{y_2 - y_1}{x_2 - x_1} = \frac{rise}{run}$$

## Special Factoring

$a^2 - b^2 = (a + b)(a - b)$

$a^2 + 2ab + b^2 = (a + b)(a + b)$

$a^2 - 2ab + b^2 = (a - b)(a - b)$

$a^3 + b^3 = (a + b)(a^2 - ab + b^2)$

$a^3 - b^3 = (a - b)(a^2 + ab + b^2)$

## Quadratic Formula

for $ax^2 + bx + c = 0$

$$x = \frac{-b \pm \sqrt{b^2 - 4ac}}{2a}$$

## Interest

**Simple Interest:**

$$I = prt$$

**Interest Formula (compounded $n$ times per year):**

$$A = p\left(1 + \frac{r}{n}\right)^{nt}$$

A = Amount after $t$ years.

p = principal

r = annual interest rate

t = time in years

I = Interest

## Trigonometric Identities

Pythagorean Theorem: $a^2 + b^2 = c^2$

$\sin \theta = \frac{opp}{hyp}$

$\cos \theta = \frac{adj}{hyp}$

$\tan \theta = \frac{opp}{adj}$

$sin^2\theta + cos^2\theta = 1$

$Density = \frac{Mass}{Volume}$

| **Central Angle** | **Inscribed Angle** | **Intersecting Chords Theorem** |
|---|---|---|
|  |  | 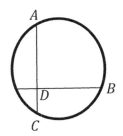 |
| $m\angle AOB = m\widehat{AB}$ | $m\angle ABC = \frac{1}{2}m\,\widehat{AC}$ | $A \cdot B = C \cdot D$ |

**Probability**

Permutations: $_nP_r = \dfrac{n!}{(n-r)!}$

Combinations: $_nC_r = \dfrac{n!}{(n-r)!r!}$

Multiplication rule (independent events): P(A and B) = P(A)·P(B)

Multiplication rule (general): P(A and B) = P(A)·P(B|A)

Addition rule: P(A or B) = P(A) + P(B) − P(A and B)

Conditional Probability: P(B|A) = $\dfrac{P(A\ and\ B)}{P(A)}$

Arithmetic Sequence: $a_n = a_1 + (n-1)d$ where $a_n$ is the $n$th term, $a_1$ is the first term, and $d$ is the common difference.

Geometric Sequence: $a_n = a_1 r^{(n-1)}$ where $a_n$ is the $n$th term, $a_1$ is the first term, and $r$ is the common ratio.

1) If 90% of $A$ is 30% of $B$, then $B$ is what percent of $A$?

A. 3%

B. 30%

C. 200%

D. 300%

2) How many possible outfit combinations come from five shirts, four slacks, and seven ties?

A. 16

B. 20

C. 70

D. 140

3) A bank is offering 8.5% simple interest on a savings account. If you deposit $12,000, how much interest will you earn in five years?

A. $1,300

B. $2,600

C. $5,100

D. $7,200

4) Which of the following could be the product of two consecutive prime numbers?

A. 2

B. 6

C. 14

D. 19

5) Which of the following lists shows the fractions in order from least to greatest?

$$\frac{3}{4}, \frac{2}{7}, \frac{3}{8}, \frac{7}{11}$$

A. $\frac{3}{8}, \frac{2}{7}, \frac{3}{4}, \frac{7}{11}$

B. $\frac{2}{7}, \frac{7}{11}, \frac{3}{8}, \frac{3}{4}$

C. $\frac{2}{7}, \frac{3}{8}, \frac{7}{11}, \frac{3}{4}$

D. $\frac{3}{8}, \frac{2}{7}, \frac{7}{11}, \frac{3}{4}$

6) What is the value of $5^5$?

A. 25

B. 125

C. 625

D. 3,125

7) 15 is What percent of 25?

A. 30%

B. 55%

C. 60%

D. 80%

8) Two third of 18 is equal to $\frac{2}{5}$ of what number?

A. 12

B. 20

C. 30

D. 60

9) The price of a car was $28,000 in 2012. In 2013, the price of that car was $18,200. What was the rate of depreciation of the price of car per year?

A. 20%

B. 30%

C. 35%

D. 40%

10) The width of a box is one third of its length. The height of the box is half of its width. If the length of the box is $24\ cm$, what is the volume of the box?

A. $72\ cm^3$

B. $144\ cm^3$

C. $288\ cm^3$

D. $768\ cm^3$

11) The marked price of a computer is $D$ dollar. Its price decreased by 25% in January and later increased by 20% in February. What is the final price of the computer in $D$ dollar?

A. $0.80\ D$

B. $0.90\ D$

C. $0.95\ D$

D. $1.20\ D$

12) A $50 shirt now selling for $38 is discounted by what percent?

A. 14%

B. 24%

C. 34%

D. 68%

13) A boat sails 90 miles south and then 120 miles east. How far is the boat from its start point?

A. 140 miles

B. 150 miles

C. 160 miles

D. 170 miles

14) The ratio of boys and girls in a class is 4: 7. If there are 77 students in the class, how many more boys should be enrolled to make the ratio 1: 1?

A. 8

B. 15

C. 21

D. 30

15) Sophia purchased a sofa for $250.50 . The sofa is regularly priced at $300. What was the percent discount Sophia received on the sofa?

A. 14.50%

B. 16.50%

C. 18%

D. 18.50%

16) The score of Emma was half as that of Ava and the score of Mia was twice that of Ava. If the score of Mia was 80, what is the score of Emma?

A. 12

B. 15

C. 20

D. 30

17) A bag contains 20 balls: four green, five black, eight blue, a brown, a red and one white. If 19 balls are removed from the bag at random, what is the probability that a brown ball has been removed?

A. $\frac{1}{9}$

B. $\frac{1}{6}$

C. $\frac{16}{17}$

D. $\frac{19}{20}$

18) How many tiles of $8\ cm^2$ is needed to cover a floor of dimension $8\ cm$ by $32\ cm$?

A. 8

B. 18

C. 32

D. 56

19) A rope weighs 800 grams per meter of length. What is the weight in kilograms of 14.4 meters of this rope? (1 kilograms = 1,000 grams)

A. $1.152\ kg$

B. $11.52\ kg$

C. $115.2\ kg$

D. $1152\ kg$

20) When a number is subtracted from 18 and the difference is divided by that number, the result is 5. What is the value of the number?

A. 1

B. 2

C. 3

D. 6

21) An angle is equal to one fourth of its supplement. What is the measure of that angle?

A. 36

B. 25

C. 15

D. 10

22) John traveled $160\ km$ in 4 hours and Alice traveled $210\ km$ in 3 hours. What is the ratio of the average speed of John to average speed of Alice?

A. $4:3$

B. $3:5$

C. $4:7$

D. $7:9$

23) The diagonal of a rectangle is 10 inches long and the height of the rectangle is 8 inches. What is the perimeter of the rectangle in inches?

A. 28

B. 26

C. 22

D. 18

24) The average of five consecutive numbers is 38. What is the smallest number?

A. 38

B. 36

C. 34

D. 12

25) Find the average of the following numbers: $12, 10, 4, 8, 11, 9$

A. 5

B. 9.5

C. 9

D. 11

26) The average weight of 20 girls in a class is $58\ kg$ and the average weight of 30 boys in the same class is $66\ kg$. What is the average weight of all the 50 students in that class?

A. 62

B. 62.8

C. 62.08

D. 62.88

27) The price of a laptop is decreased by 20% to $420. What is its original price?

A. $480

B. $500

C. $525

D. $550

28) What is the median of these numbers? 5, 10, 14, 9,19, 6 16

A. 9

B. 10

C. 14

D. 16

29) A taxi driver earns $9 per 1 −hour work. If he works 10 hours a day and in 1 hour he uses 2 −liters petrol with price $1 for 1 −liter. How much money does he earn in one day?

A. $90

B. $88

C. $70

D. $60

30) The radius of the following cylinder is 8 inches and its height is 16 inches. What is the surface area of the cylinder in square inches? ($\pi = 3.14$)

A. 423.4

B. 876.12

C. 928.28

D. 1,205.76

31) How long does a 390−miles trip take moving at 60 miles per hour ($mph$)?

A. 6 hours

B. 6 hours and 50 minutes

C. 6 hours and 30 minutes

D. 8 hours and 35 minutes

32) In the $xy$-plane, the point $(1, 2)$ and $(-1, 6)$ are on line $A$. Which of the following points could also be on line $A$? (Select one or more answer choices)

A. $(-1, 2)$

B. $(5, 7)$

C. $(3, 4)$

D. $(3, -2)$

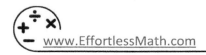

33) In 1999, the average worker's income increased $2,000 per year starting from $23,000 annual salary. Which equation represents income greater than average? ($I$ = income, $x$ = number of years after 1999)

A. $I > 2,000x + 23,000$

B. $I > -2,000x + 23,000$

C. $I < -2,000x + 23,000$

D. $I < 2,000x - 23,000$

34) The price of a sofa is decreased by 18% to $451. What was its original price?

A. $480

B. $535

C. $550

D. $680

35) Right triangle $ABC$ has two legs of lengths $3\ cm\ (AB)$ and $4\ cm\ (AC)$. What is the length of the third side $(BC)$?

A. $15\ cm$

B. $14\ cm$

C. $8\ cm$

D. $5\ cm$

36) If 50% of a class are girls, and 30% of girls play tennis, what percent of the class play tennis?

A. 10%

B. 15%

C. 20%

D. 40%

37) In five successive hours, a car traveled 40 $km$, 45 $km$, 50 $km$, 35 $km$ and 55 $km$. In the next five hours, it traveled with an average speed of 75 $km$ per hour. Find the total distance the car traveled in 10 hours.

A. 425 $km$

B. 550 $km$

C. 600 $km$

D. 670 $km$

38) The area of a circle is less than $64\pi$. Which of the following can be the circumference of the circle?

A. $12\pi$

B. $16\pi$

C. $24\pi$

D. $32\pi$

39) Which of the following values for $x$ and $y$ satisfy the following system of equations?

$$\begin{cases} x + 4y = 10 \\ 5x + 5y = 20 \end{cases}$$

A. $x = -2, y = -2$

B. $x = 2, y - 3$

C. $x = 2, y = 2$

D. $x = 3, y = -2$

40) A chemical solution contains 6% alcohol. If there is 42 $ml$ of alcohol, what is the volume of the solution?

A. 140 $ml$

B. 380 $ml$

C. 700 $ml$

D. 1,100 $ml$

IF YOU FINISH BEFORE TIME IS CALLED, YOU MAY CHECK YOUR WORK ON THIS SECTION ONLY. DO NOT TURN TO OTHER SECTION IN THE TEST.    **STOP**

# TASC Mathematics

# Practice Test

## Part 2 (Non-Calculator)

**Total number of questions:** 12

**Total time for Part 1 (Calculator):** 50 Minutes

# You may NOT use a calculator on this part.

41) $32 - 3 \times (6) - [8 + 16 \times (-5)] \div 2 - 12 = ?$

42) What is the area of an isosceles right triangle that has one leg that measures 8?

43) The average of $11, 13, 18$ and $x$ is 20. What is the value of $x$?

44) The perimeter of the trapezoid below is 62. What is its area?

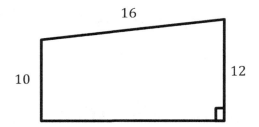

45) From last year, the price of gasoline has increased from $2.50 per gallon to $2.75 per gallon. The new price is what percent of the original price?

46) If $2x - 6 = 6.5$, What is the value of $-3x + 20$ ?

47) If $75\%$ of a class are girls, and $\frac{1}{3}$ of girls take drawing class this semester, what percent of the class are girls who take drawing class this semester?

48) If $\frac{x-4}{6} = N$ and $N = 8$, what is the value of $x$?

49) Jason purchased a laptop for $529.72. The laptop is regularly priced at $646.00. What was the percent discount Jason received on the laptop?

50) What is the value of $f(-2)$ for the following function $f$?

$$f(x) = 2x^2 + 4x$$

51) If the ratio of $5a$ to $2b$ is $\frac{1}{6}$, what is the ratio of $a$ to $b$?

52) A construction company is building a wall. The company can build $40\ cm$ of the wall per minute. After 50 minutes $\frac{2}{3}$ of the wall is completed. How many meters is the wall?

IF YOU FINISH BEFORE TIME IS CALLED, YOU MAY CHECK YOUR WORK ON THIS SECTION ONLY. DO NOT TURN TO OTHER SECTION IN THE TEST.    **STOP**

# TASC Mathematics Practice Test Answers and Explanations

Now, it's time to review your results to see where you went wrong and what areas you need to improve!

| TASC Practice Test Answer key | | | | | | | | |
|---|---|---|---|---|---|---|---|---|
| 1 | D | 16 | C | 31 | C | 41 | 38 |
| 2 | D | 17 | D | 32 | D | 42 | 32 |
| 3 | C | 18 | C | 33 | A | 43 | 38 |
| 4 | B | 19 | B | 34 | C | 44 | 264 |
| 5 | C | 20 | C | 35 | D | 45 | 110 |
| 6 | D | 21 | A | 36 | B | 46 | 1.25 |
| 7 | C | 22 | C | 37 | C | 47 | 25 |
| 8 | C | 23 | A | 38 | A | 48 | 52 |
| 9 | C | 24 | B | 39 | C | 49 | 18 |
| 10 | D | 25 | C | 40 | C | 50 | 0 |
| 11 | B | 26 | B | | | 51 | 0.06 |
| 12 | B | 27 | C | | | 52 | 30 |
| 13 | B | 28 | B | | | | |
| 14 | C | 29 | C | | | | |
| 15 | B | 30 | D | | | | |

# TASC Mathematics Practice Test

## Answers and Explanations

**1) Choice D is correct**

Write the equation and solve for $B$: $0.90A = 0.30\,B$, divide both sides by 0.30, then:

$\frac{0.90}{0.30}A = B$, therefore: $B = 3A$, and $B$ is 3 times of $A$ or it's 300% of $A$.

**2) Choice D is correct**

To find the number of possible outfit combinations, multiply number of options for each factor:

$5 \times 4 \times 7 = 140$

**3) Choice C is correct**

Use simple interest formula: $I = prt$ $(I = interest, p = principal, r = rate, t = time)$

$I = (12,000)(0.085)(5) = 5,100$

**4) Choices B is correct**

Some of prime numbers are: $2, 3, 5, 7, 11, 13$. Find the product of two consecutive prime numbers: $2 \times 3 = 6$ (bingo!), $3 \times 5 = 15$ (not in the options), $5 \times 7 = 35$ (not in the options), $7 \times 11 = 77$ (not in the options)

**5) Choice C is correct**

Let's compare each fraction: $\frac{2}{7} < \frac{3}{8} < \frac{7}{11} < \frac{3}{4}$, Only choice C provides the right order.

**6) Choice D is correct**

$5^5 = 5 \times 5 \times 5 \times 5 \times 5 = 3,125$

**7) Choice C is correct**

$x = \dfrac{15}{25} = 0.6 = 60\%$

**8) Choice C is correct**

Let $x$ be the number. Write the equation and solve for $x$.

$\frac{2}{3} \times 18 = \frac{2}{5}x \rightarrow \frac{2 \times 18}{3} = \frac{2x}{5}$ , use cross multiplication to solve for $x$.

$$5 \times 36 = 2x \times 3 \rightarrow 180 = 6x \rightarrow x = 30$$

**9) Choice C is correct**

Use this formula: Percent of Change: $\frac{New\ Value - Old\ Value}{Old\ Value} \times 100\%$

$\frac{28,000 - 18,200}{28,000} \times 100\% = -35\%$. The negative sign means that the price decreased

**10) Choice D is correct**

If the length of the box is 24, then the width of the box is one third of it, 8, and the height of the box is 4 (half of the width). The volume of the box is: $V = lwh = (24)(8)(4) = 768$

**11) Choice B is correct**

To find the discount, multiply the number by $(100\% - rate\ of\ discount)$.

Therefore, for the first discount we get: $(D)(100\% - 25\%) = (D)(0.75) = 0.75\ D$

For increase of 20%: $(0.75D)(100\% + 20\%) = (0.75\ D)(1.20) = 0.90\ D = 90\%\ of\ D$

**12) Choice B is correct**

Use the formula for Percent of Change: $\frac{New\ Value - Old\ Value}{Old\ Value} \times 100\%$

$\frac{38 - 50}{50} \times 100\% = \frac{-12}{50} \times 100\% = -24\%$ (negative sign here means that the new price is less than old price).

**13) Choice B is correct**

Use the information provided in the question to draw the shape.

Use Pythagorean Theorem: $a^2 + b^2 = c^2$

$90^2 + 120^2 = c^2 \Rightarrow 8,100 + 14,400 = c^2 \Rightarrow 22,500 = c^2 \Rightarrow c = 150$

120 miles

90 miles

**14) Choice C is correct**

The ratio of boy to girls is $4:7$. Therefore, there are 4 boys out of 11 students. To find the answer, first divide the total number of students by 11, then multiply the result by 4.

$77 \div 11 = 7 \Rightarrow 4 \times 7 = 28$. There are 28 boys and 49 $(77 - 28)$ girls. So, 21 more boys should be enrolled to make the ratio $1:1$

**15) Choice B is correct**

The question is this: 250.50 is what percent of 300?

Use percent formula: $part = \frac{percent}{100} \times whole$

$250.50 = \frac{percent}{100} \times 300 \Rightarrow 250.50 = \frac{percent \times 300}{100} \Rightarrow 25050 = percent \times 300 \Rightarrow$

$percent = \frac{25050}{300} = 83.5$

250.50 is 83.5% of 300. Therefore, the discount is: $100\% - 83.5\% = 16.50\%$

**16) Choice C is correct**

If the score of Mia was 80, therefore the score of Ava is 40. Since, the score of Emma was half as that of Ava, therefore, the score of Emma is 20.

**17) Choice D is correct**

If 19 balls are removed from the bag at random, there will be one ball in the bag. The probability of choosing a brown ball is 1 out of 20. Therefore, the probability of not choosing a brown ball is 19 out of 20 and the probability of having not a brown ball after removing 19 balls is the same.

**18) Choice C is correct**

The area of the floor is: $8\ cm \times 32\ cm = 256\ cm^2$, The number of tiles needed $= 256 \div 8 = 32$

**19) Choice B is correct**

The weight of 14.4 meters of this rope is: $14.4 \times 800\ g = 11,520\ g$

$1\ kg = 1,000$ g, therefore, $11,520\ g \div 1,000 = 11.52\ kg$

**20) Choice C is correct**

Let $x$ be the number. Write the equation and solve for $x$. $(18 - x) \div x = 5$, Multiply both sides by $x$: $(18 - x) = 5x$, Then add $x$ both sides: $18 = 6x$, now divide both sides by 6: $x = 3$

**21) Choice A is correct**

The sum of supplement angles is 180. Let $x$ be that angle. Therefore, $x + 4x = 180$

$5x = 180$, divide both sides by 5: $x = 36$

**22) Choice C is correct**

The average speed of john is: $160 \div 4 = 40$, The average speed of Alice is: $210 \div 3 = 70$,

Write the ratio and simplify. $40 : 70 \Rightarrow 4 : 7$

**23) Choice A is correct**

Let $x$ be the width of the rectangle. Use Pythagorean Theorem: $a^2 + b^2 = c^2$

$x^2 + 8^2 = 10^2 \Rightarrow x^2 + 64 = 100 \Rightarrow x^2 = 100 - 64 = 36 \Rightarrow x = 6$

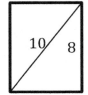

Perimeter of the rectangle $= 2\,(length\ +\ width) = 2\,(8 + 6) = 2\,(14) = 28$

**24) Choice B is correct**

Let $x$ be the smallest number. Then, these are the numbers:

$x, x + 1, x + 2, x + 3, x + 4$

$average\ =\ \dfrac{sum\ of\ terms}{number\ of\ terms} \Rightarrow 38 = \dfrac{x+(x+1)+(x+2)+(x+3)+(x+4)}{5} \Rightarrow 38 = \dfrac{5x+10}{5} \Rightarrow$

$$190 = 5x + 10 \Rightarrow 180 = 5x \Rightarrow x = 36$$

**25) Choice C is correct**

$average = \dfrac{sum\ of\ terms}{number\ of\ terms} = \dfrac{12+10+4+8+11+9}{6} = \dfrac{54}{6} = 9$

**26) Choice B is correct**

$average = \dfrac{sum\ of\ terms}{number\ of\ terms}$

The sum of the weight of all girls is: $20 \times 58 = 1,160 \ kg$, The sum of the weight of all boys is: $30 \times 66 = 1,980 \ kg$, The sum of the weight of all students is: $1,160 + 1,980 = 3,140 \ kg$. $average = \frac{3,140}{50} = 62.8$

**27) Choice C is correct**

Let $x$ be the original price.

If the price of a laptop is decreased by 20% to \$420, then: $80\% \ of \ x = 420 \Rightarrow 0.80x = 420$ $\Rightarrow x = 420 \div 0.80 = 525$

**28) Choice B is correct**

Write the numbers in order: $5, 6, 9, 10, 14, 16, 19$. Since we have 7 numbers (7 is odd), then the median is the number in the middle, which is 10.

**29) Choice C is correct**

$\$9 \times 10 = \$90$,         Petrol use:      $10 \times 2 = 20$ liters

Petrol cost:     $20 \times \$1 = \$20$, Money earned:        $\$90 - \$20 = \$70$

**30) Choice D is correct**

Surface Area of a cylinder $= 2\pi r \ (r + h)$,

The radius of the cylinder is 8 inches and its height is 12 inches. $\pi$ is 3.14. Then:

Surface Area of a cylinder $= 2 \ (3.14) \ (8) \ (8 + 16) = 1,205.76$

**31) Choice C is correct**

Use distance formula: $Distance = Rate \times time \Rightarrow 390 = 60 \times T$,  divide both sides by 60: $\frac{390}{60} = T \Rightarrow T = 6.5$ hours. Change hours to minutes for the decimal part. $0.5$ hours $= 0.5 \times 60 = 30$ minutes

**32) Choice D is correct**

The equation of a line is in the form of $y = mx + b$, where $m$ is the slope of the line and $b$ is the $y$−intercept of the line. Two points $(1, 2)$ and $(−1, 6)$ are on line $A$. Therefore, the slope of the line $A$ is: $slope\ of\ line\ A = \frac{y_2 - y_1}{x_2 - x_1} = \frac{6-2}{-1-1} = \frac{4}{-2} = -2$

The slope of line $A$ is $−2$. Thus, the formula of the line $A$ is: $y = mx + b = -2x + b$, choose a point and plug in the values of $x$ and $y$ in the equation to solve for $b$. Let's choose point $(1, 2)$. Then: $y = -2x + b \rightarrow 2 = -2(1) + b \rightarrow b = 2 + 2 = 4$. The equation of line $A$ is: $y = -2x + 4$

Now, let's review the choices provided:

A. $(−1, 2)$     $y = -2x + 4 \rightarrow 2 = -2(-1) + 4 = 6$     This is not true.

B. $(5, 7)$     $y = -2x + 4 \rightarrow 7 = -2(5) + 4 = -6$     This is not true.

C. $(3, 4)$     $y = -2x + 4 \rightarrow 4 = -2(3) + 4 = -2$     This is not true.

D. $(3, −2)$     $y = -2x + 4 \rightarrow -2 = -2(3) + 4 = -2$     This is true!

**33) Choice A is correct**

Let $x$ be the number of years. Therefore, $2,000 per year equals $2,000x$. starting from $23,000 annual salary means you should add that amount to $2,000x$. Income more than that is: $I > 2,000x + 23,000$

**34) Choice C is correct**

Let $x$ be the original price. If the price of the sofa is decreased by 18% to $451, then: $82\%\ of\ x = 451 \Rightarrow 0.82x = 451 \Rightarrow x = 451 \div 0.82 = 550$

**35) Choice D is correct**

Use Pythagorean Theorem: $a^2 + b^2 = c^2$

$3^2 + 4^2 = c^2 \Rightarrow 9 + 16 = c^2 \Rightarrow 25 = c^2 \Rightarrow c = 5$

**36) Choice B is correct**

The percent of girls playing tennis is: $50\% \times 30\% = 0.50 \times 0.30 = 0.15 = 15\%$

**37) Choice C is correct**

Add the first 5 numbers. $40 + 45 + 50 + 35 + 55 = 225$

To find the distance traveled in the next 5 hours, multiply the average by number of hours.

$Distance = Average \times Rate = 75 \times 5 = 375$

Add both numbers. $375 + 225 = 600$

**38) Choice A is correct**

Area of the circle is less than $16\pi$. Use the formula of areas of circles.

$Area = \pi r^2 \Rightarrow 64\pi > \pi r^2 \Rightarrow 64 > r^2 \Rightarrow r < 8$

Radius of the circle is less than 8. Let's put 8 for the radius. Now, use the circumference formula:

$Circumference = 2\pi r = 2\pi (8) = 16\pi$

Since the radius of the circle is less than 8. Then, the circumference of the circle must be less than $16\pi$. Only choice A is less than $16\pi$.

**39) Choice C is correct**

$\begin{cases} x + 4y = 10 \\ 5x + 5y = 20 \end{cases} \rightarrow$  Multiply the top equation by $-5$ then,

$\begin{cases} -5x - 20y = -50 \\ \phantom{-}5x + 5y = 20 \end{cases} \rightarrow$  Add two equations

$-15y = -30 \rightarrow y = 2$ , plug in the value of $y$ into the first equation

$x + 4y = 10 \rightarrow x + 4(2) = 10 \rightarrow x + 8 = 10$. Subtract 12 from both sides of the equation. Then: $x + 8 = 10 \rightarrow x = 2$

**40) Choice C is correct**

$6\%$ of the volume of the solution is alcohol. Let $x$ be the volume of the solution.

Then: $6\% \ of \ x = 42 \ ml \Rightarrow 0.06x = 42 \Rightarrow x = 42 \div 0.06 = 700$

**41) The answer is 38**

Use PEMDAS (order of operation): $32 - 3 \times (6) - [8 + 16 \times (-5)] \div 2 - 12 = 32 - 3 \times (6) - (-72) \div 2 - 12 = 32 - 18 - (-72) \div 2 - 12 = 32 - 18 - (-36) - 12 = 32 - 18 + 36 - 12 = 38$

**42) The answer is 32**

First draw an isosceles triangle. Remember that two sides of the triangle are equal.

Let put $a$ for the legs. Then:

Isosceles right triangle

$a = 8 \Rightarrow$ area of the triangle is $= \frac{1}{2}(8 \times 8) = \frac{64}{2} = 32$

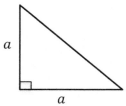

**43) The answer is 38**

$average = \frac{sum\ of\ terms}{number\ of\ terms} \Rightarrow 20 = \frac{11+13+18+x}{4} \Rightarrow 80 = 42 + x \Rightarrow x = 38$

**44) The answer is 264**

The perimeter of the trapezoid is 62.

Therefore, the missing side (height) is $= 62 - 16 - 10 - 12 = 24$

Area of a trapezoid: $A = \frac{1}{2}h\ (b_1 + b_2) = \frac{1}{2}(24)(10 + 12\ ) = \frac{1}{2}(24)(22\ ) = \frac{1}{2} \times 528 = 264$

**45) The answer is 110**

$\frac{2.75}{2.50} = 110$

**46) The answer is 1. 25**

$2x - 6 = 6.5 \rightarrow 2x = 6.5 + 6 \rightarrow 2x = 12.5 \rightarrow x = \frac{12.5}{2} = 6.25$

Then: $-3x + 20 = -3(6.25) + 20 = -18.75 + 20 = 1.25$

**47) The answer is 25**

The percent of girls take drawing class is: $75\% \times \frac{1}{3} = 25\%$

**48) The answer is 52**

Since $N = 8$, substitute 8 for $N$ in the equation $\frac{x-4}{6} = N$, which gives $\frac{x-4}{6} = 8$. Multiplying both sides of $\frac{x-4}{6} = 8$ by 6 gives $x - 4 = 48$ and then adding 4 to both sides of $x - 4 = 48$, then: $x = 52$.

**49) The answer is 18**

The question is this: 529.72 is what percent of 646? Use percent formula:

$$part = \frac{percent}{100} \times whole. \quad 529.72 = \frac{percent}{100} \times 646 \Rightarrow 529.72 = \frac{percent \times 646}{100} \Rightarrow$$

$$52,972 = percent \times 646 \Rightarrow percent = \frac{52,972}{646} = 82$$

529.72 is 82% of 646. Therefore, the discount is: $100\% - 82\% = 18\%$

**50) The answer is 0**

The input value is $-2$. Then: $x = -2$, $f(x) = 2(-2)^2 + 4(-2) = 2(4) - 8 = 8 - 8 = 0$

**51) The answer is $\frac{1}{15}$ or $0.06$**

Write the ratio of $5a$ to $2b$. $\frac{5a}{2b} = \frac{1}{6}$

Use cross multiplication and then simplify. $5a \times 6 = 2b \times 1 \rightarrow 30a = 2b \rightarrow a = \frac{2b}{30} = \frac{b}{15}$

Now, find the ratio of $a$ to $b$. $\frac{a}{b} = \frac{\frac{b}{15}}{b} \rightarrow \frac{b}{15} \div b = \frac{b}{15} \times \frac{1}{b} = \frac{b}{15b} = \frac{1}{15} = 0.06$

**52) The answer is 30**

The rate of construction company$= \frac{40\ cm}{1\ min} = 40\ \frac{cm}{min}$

Height of the wall after 50 minutes $= \frac{40\ cm}{1\ min} \times 50\ min = 2,000\ cm$

Let $x$ be the height of wall, then $\frac{2}{3}x = 2,000cm \rightarrow x = \frac{3 \times 2,000}{2} \rightarrow x = 3,000\ cm = 30\ m$

# www.EffortlessMath.com

... So Much More Online!

✓ FREE Math lessons

✓ More Math learning books!

✓ Mathematics Worksheets

✓ Online Math Tutors

**Need a PDF version of this book?**

Visit www.EffortlessMath.com

# Receive the PDF version of this book or get another FREE book!

Thank you for using our Book!

Do you LOVE this book?

Then, you can get the PDF version of this book or another book absolutely FREE!

Please email us at:

info@EffortlessMath.com

for details.

# Author's Final Note

I hope you enjoyed reading this book. You've made it through the book! Great job!

First of all, thank you for purchasing this study guide. I know you could have picked any number of books to help you prepare for your TASC Math test, but you picked this book and for that I am extremely grateful.

It took me years to write this study guide for the TASC Math because I wanted to prepare a comprehensive TASC Math study guide to help test takers make the most effective use of their valuable time while preparing for the test.

After teaching and tutoring math for over a decade, I've gathered my personal notes and lessons to develop this study guide. It is my greatest hope that the lessons in this book could help you prepare for your test successfully.

If you have any questions, please contact me at reza@effortlessmath.com and I will be glad to assist. Your feedback will help me to greatly improve the quality of my books in the future and make this book even better. Furthermore, I expect that I have made a few minor errors somewhere in this study guide. If you think this to be the case, please let me know so I can fix the issue as soon as possible.

If you enjoyed this book and found some benefit in reading this, I'd like to hear from you and hope that you could take a quick minute to post a review on the book's Amazon page. To leave your valuable feedback, please visit: rebrand.ly/789ff

Or scan this QR code.

I personally go over every single review, to make sure my books really are reaching out and helping students and test takers. Please help me help TASC Math test takers, by leaving a review!

I wish you all the best in your future success!


Reza Nazari

Math teacher and author

26867851R00138